origami
on the
move

cars, trucks, ships, planes & more

Duy Nguyen

Sterling Publishing Co., Inc.

New York

Design by Judy Morgan
Edited by Claire Bazinet

Library of Congress Cataloging-in-Publication Data

Nguyen, Duy.
  Origami on the move : cars, trucks, ships, planes & more /
Duy Nguyen.
      p. cm.
  Includes bibliographical references and index.
  ISBN 1-4027-1933-7 (alk. paper)
  1. Origami. 2. Transportation in art. I. Bazinet, Claire. II. Title.

TT870.N4875 2005
736'.982--dc22

                                          2005001459

10 9 8 7 6 5 4 3 2

Published by Sterling Publishing Co., Inc.
387 Park Avenue South, New York, NY 10016
© 2005 by Duy Nguyen
Distributed in Canada by Sterling Publishing
c/o Canadian Manda Group, 165 Dufferin Street, Toronto, Ontario, Canada M6K 3H6
Distributed in Great Britain and Europe by Chris Lloyd at Orca Book
Services, Stanley House, Fleets Lane, Poole BH15 3AJ, England
Distributed in Australia by Capricorn Link (Australia) Pty. Ltd.
P.O. Box 704, Windsor, NSW 2756, Australia

Sterling ISBN 1-4027-1933-7

For information about custom editions, special sales, premium
and corporate purchases, please contact Sterling Special Sales
Department at 800-805-5489 or specialsales@sterlingpub.com.

Contents

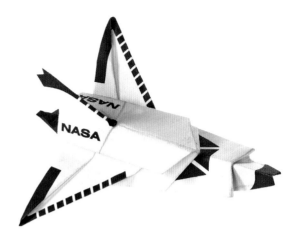

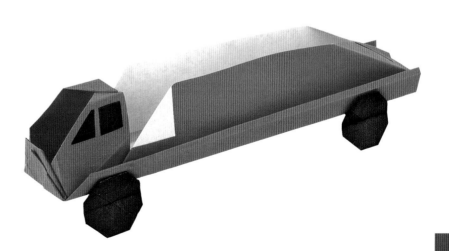

Preface

Years ago, when I began to fold origami, it was a struggle. I would look at even the simplest folds given at the beginning of the book again and again. Bur I also looked ahead, at the diagram showing the next step of whatever project I was folding, to see how it *should* look. That was the right thing to do. Looking ahead at the "next step," the result of a fold, is a very good way for a beginner to learn origami.

You will easily pick up this and other learning techniques as you follow the step-by-step directions given here for making over a dozen vehicles of all kinds, from a space shuttle to an aircraft carrier with a full complement of carrier jets. Wherever your interests lie, the variety of projects here will both challenge and satisfy. And with these under your belt, there's nothing to stop you from trying to create your own original cars, trucks, planes, ships, and whatever other mode of transport you see or can imagine.

Duy Nguyen

Basic Instructions

Paper: Paper used in traditional origami is thin, keeps a crease well, and folds flat. Packets of specially designed sheets, about 6 and 8 inches square (15 and 21 cm), are available in various colors. A few of the projects given here call for rectangular size paper, but this shouldn't be a problem. You can use plain white, solid-color, or even wrapping paper with a design only on one side and cut the paper to size. Be aware, though, that some papers stretch slightly in length or width, which can cause folding problems, while others tear easily.

Beginners, or those concerned about getting their fingers to work tight folds, might consider using larger paper sizes. Regular paper may be too heavy to allow the many tight folds needed in creating more traditional, origami figures, but fine for larger versions of these intriguing projects. So sit down, select some paper, and begin to fold and enjoy the wonderful art that is origami.

Glue: Use an easy-flowing but not loose paper glue. Use it sparingly; don't soak the paper. On delicate projects, a flat tooth-pick makes a good applicator. Be sure to allow the glued form time to dry. Avoid stick glue which, if it has become overly dry, can crease or damage your figure.

Technique: Fold with care. Position the paper, especially at corners, precisely and line edges up before creasing. Once you are sure of the fold, use a fingernail to make a clean, flat crease.

For more complex folds, create "construction lines." Fold and unfold, using simple mountain and valley folds, to pre-crease. This creates guidelines, and the finished fold is more likely to match the one shown in the book. Folds that look different, because the angles are slightly different, can throw you off. Don't get discouraged with your first efforts. In time, what your mind can create, your fingers can fashion.

Symbols & Lines

| Fold lines | valley | - - - - - - - - - - | Fold then unfold | |
| | mountain | - · - · - · - · - | | |

| Cut line | ┼┼┼┼┼┼┼┼┼┼┼ | Pleat fold (repeated folding) | |

| Turn over or rotate | | Crease line | |

Squaring-Off Paper

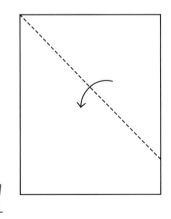

1

Take a rectangular sheet of paper and valley fold it diagonally to opposite edge.

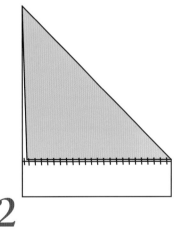

2

Cut off excess on long side as shown.

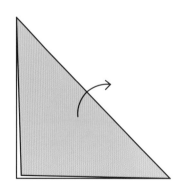

3

Unfold, and sheet is square.

Basic Folds

Kite Fold

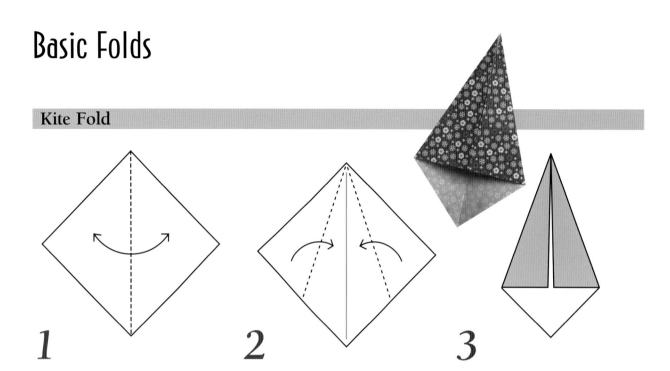

1
Fold and unfold a square diagonally, making a center crease.

2
Fold both sides in to the center crease.

3
This is a kite form.

Valley Fold ------------------

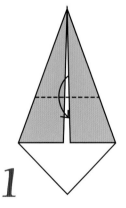
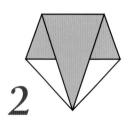

1
Here, using the kite, fold form toward you (forwards), making a "valley."

2
This fold forward is a valley fold.

Mountain Fold –·–·–·–·–·–

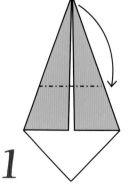
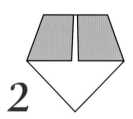

1
Here, using the kite, fold form away from you (backwards), making a "mountain."

2
This fold backwards is a mountain fold.

6

Inside Reverse Fold

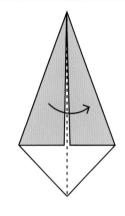

1

Starting here with a kite, valley fold kite closed.

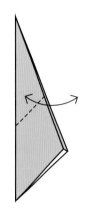

2

Valley fold as marked to crease, then unfold.

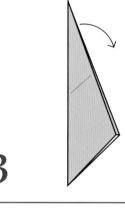

3

Pull tip in direction of arrow.

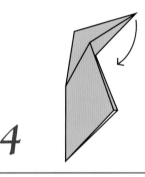

4

Appearance before completion.

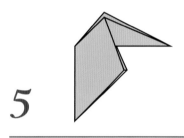

5

You've made an inside reverse fold.

Outside Reverse Fold

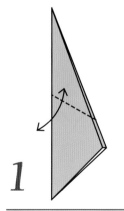

1

Using closed kite, valley fold, unfold.

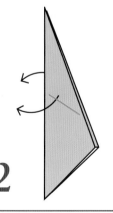

2

Fold inside out, as shown by arrows.

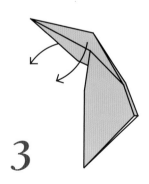

3

Appearance before completion.

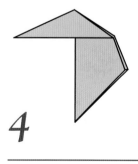

4

You've made an outside reverse fold.

Basic Folds

Pleat Fold

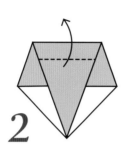

1

Here, using the kite, valley fold.

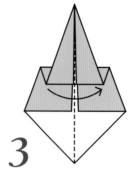

2

Valley fold back again.

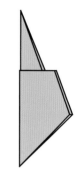

3

This is a pleat. Valley fold in half.

4

You've made a pleat fold.

Pleat Fold Reverse

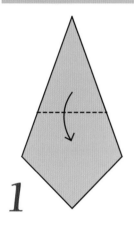

1

Here, using the kite form backwards, valley fold.

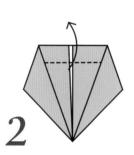

2

Valley fold back again for pleat.

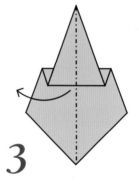

3

Mountain fold form in half.

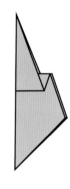

4

This is a pleat fold reverse.

Squash Fold I

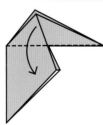

1

Using inside reverse, valley fold one side.

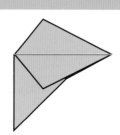

2

This is a squash fold I.

Basic Folds

Squash Fold II

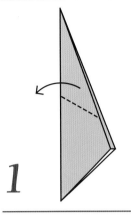

1

Using closed kite form, valley fold.

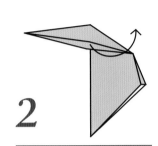

2

Open in direction of the arrow.

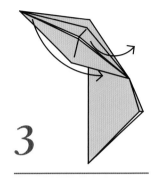

3

Appearance before completion.

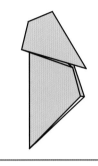

4

You've made a squash fold II.

Inside Crimp Fold

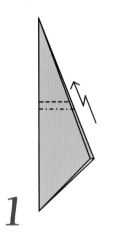

1

Here, using closed kite form, pleat fold.

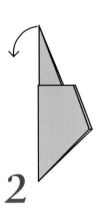

2

Pull tip in direction of the arrow.

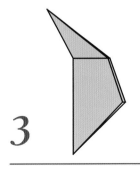

3

This is an inside crimp fold.

Outside Crimp Fold

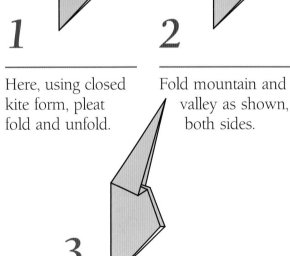

1

Here, using closed kite form, pleat fold and unfold.

2

Fold mountain and valley as shown, both sides.

3

This is an outside crimp fold.

Base Folds

Base folds are basic forms that do not in themselves produce origami, but serve as a basis, or jumping-off point, for a number of creative origami figures—some quite complex. As when beginning other crafts, learning to fold these base folds is not the most exciting part of origami. They are, however, easy to do, and will help you with your technique. They also quickly become rote, so much so that you can do many using different-colored papers while you are watching television or your mind is elsewhere. With completed base folds handy, if you want to quickly work up a form or are suddenly inspired with an idea for an original, unique figure, you can select an appropriate base fold and swiftly bring a new creation to life.

Base Fold I

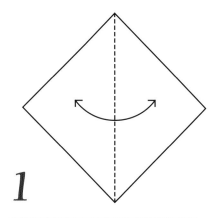

1

Fold and unfold in direction of arrow.

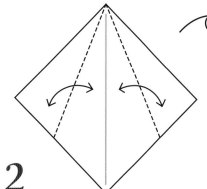

2

Fold both sides in to center crease, then unfold. Rotate.

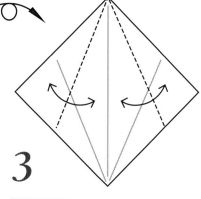

3

Fold both sides in to center crease, then unfold.

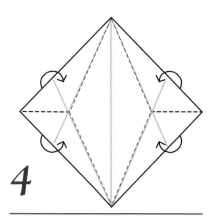

4

Pinch corners of square together and fold inward.

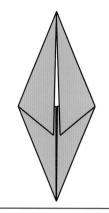

5

Completed Base Fold I.

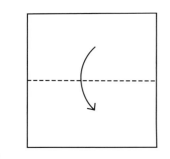

1

Valley fold.

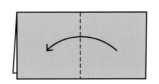

2

Valley fold.

3

Squash fold.

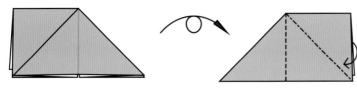

4

Turn over to other side.

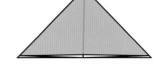

5

Squash fold.

6

Completed Base Fold II.

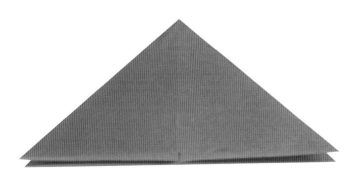

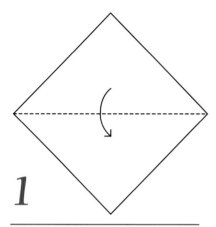

1

Valley fold.

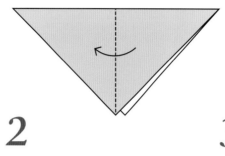

2

Valley fold.

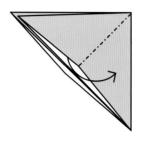

3

Squash fold.

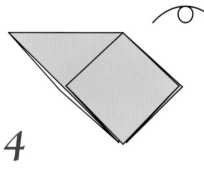

4

Turn over.

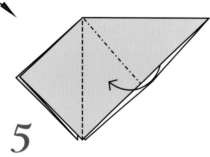

5

Squash fold.

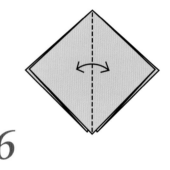

6

Valley fold, unfold.

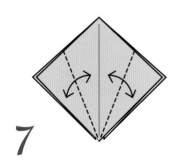

7

Valley folds, unfold.

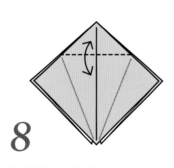

8

Valley fold, unfold.

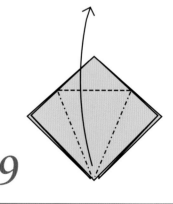

9

Pull in direction of arrow, folding inward at sides.

Base Folds

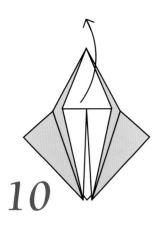

10

Appearance before
completion of fold.

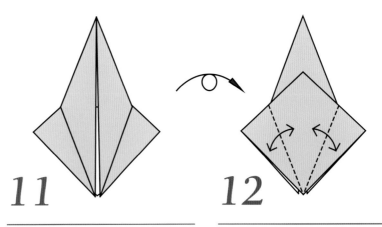

11

Fold completed. Turn over.

12

Valley folds, unfold.

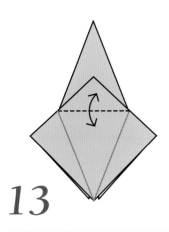

13

Valley fold, unfold.

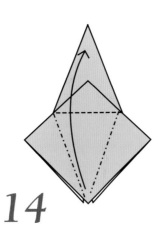

14

Repeat, again pulling in
direction of arrow.

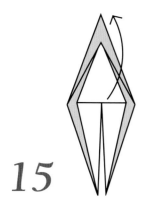

15

Appearance before
completion.

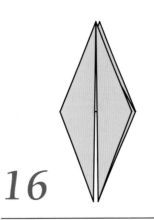

16

Completed Base Fold III.

Russian MiG-21

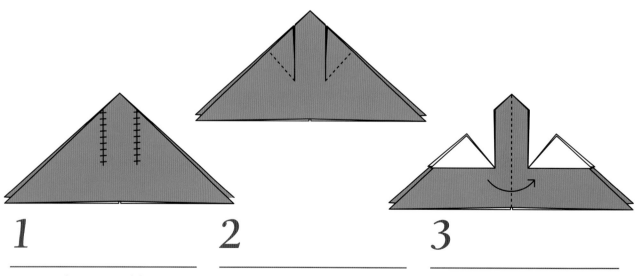

1

Start with Base Fold II. Make cuts as shown.

2

Outside reverse fold all four corners.

3

Valley fold both sides.

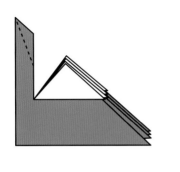

4

Valley fold both sides.

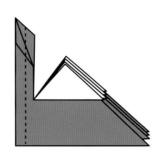

5

Valley folds.

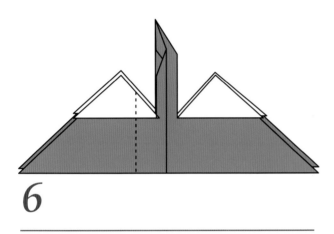

6

Valley fold both sides.

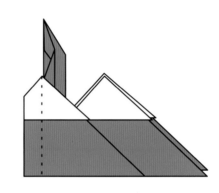

7

Valley folds.

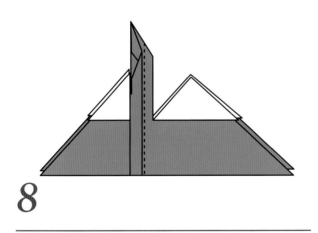

8

Valley fold both sides.

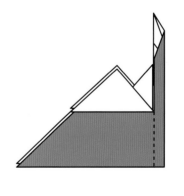

9

Valley folds.

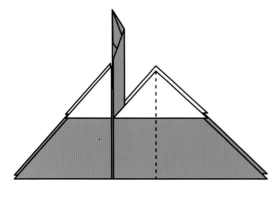

10

Valley fold both front and back.

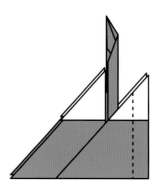

11

Valley fold both sides.

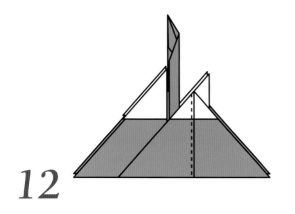

12

Valley fold both sides.

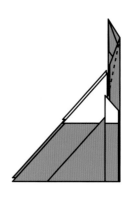

13

Valley folds.

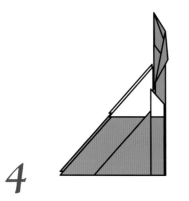

14

Rotate.

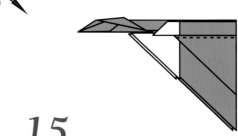

15

Valley fold wings front and back to balance.

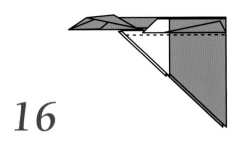

16

Valley fold and balance wings to sides.

17

Add coloring if you wish.

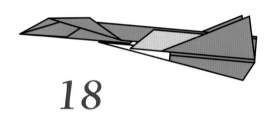

18

Completed Russian MiG-21.

Front View

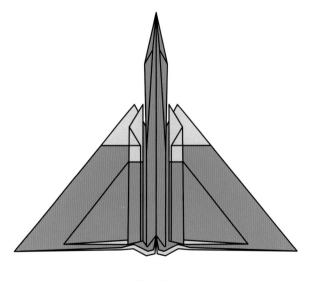

Overhead View

F-16 Falcon

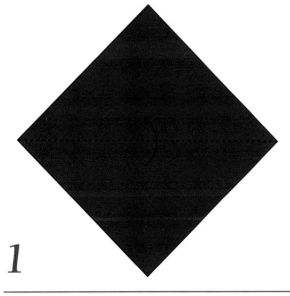

1

Valley fold in half.

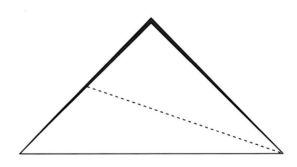

2

Valley fold.

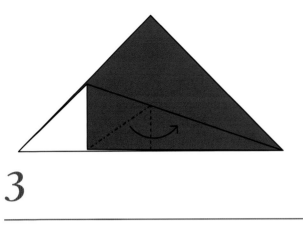

3

Pull in direction of arrow, squash fold.

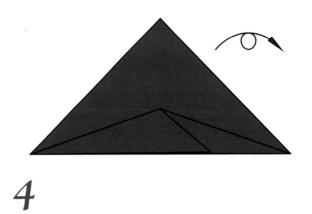

4

Turn over to other side.

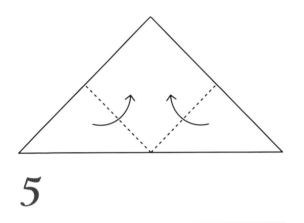

5

Valley folds.

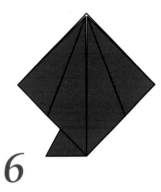

6

Inside reverse folds.

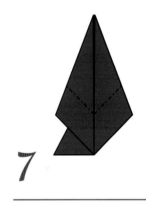

7

Inside reverse folds.

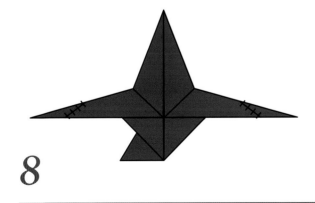

8

Make cuts to front layers only, then valley fold cut parts.

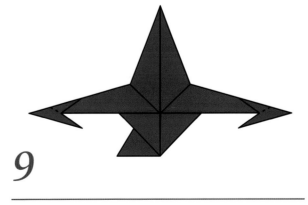

9

Valley fold both sides.

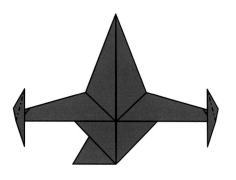

10

Inside reverse folds, left and right, as shown.

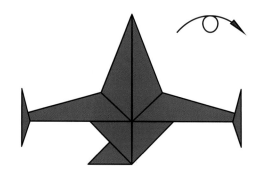

11

Turn over to other side.

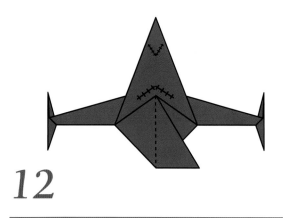

12

Cuts to front layer only, as shown, and Valley fold tail fin.

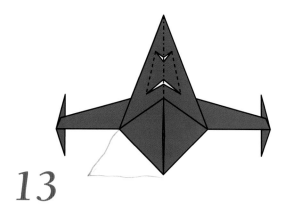

13

Valley fold in half (mountain fold cut flap). Rotate.

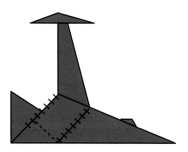

14

Cuts and valley fold cut parts.

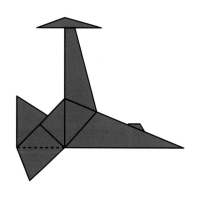

15

Valley fold outward, balancing sides.

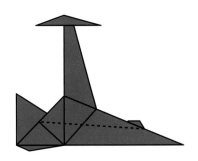

16

Valley folds to side.

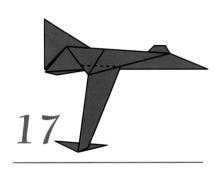

17

Valley fold to balance wings.

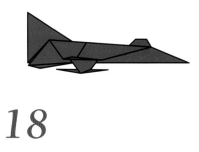

18

Add color.

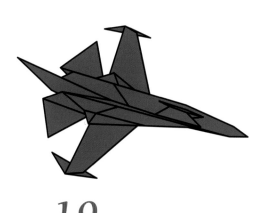

19

Completed F-16 Falcon.

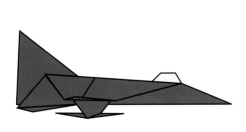

SideView

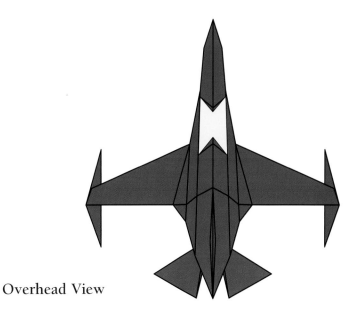

Overhead View

F-16 Falcon

Phantom

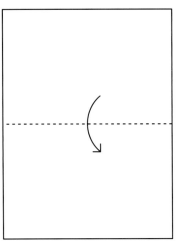

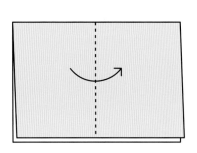

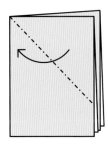

1

Start with a full sheet (8.5" by 11"). Valley fold in half.

2

Valley fold.

3

Squash fold.

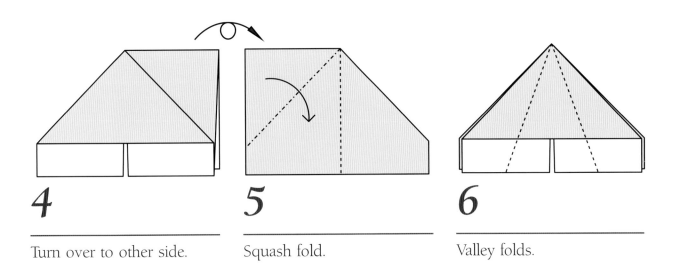

4

Turn over to other side.

5

Squash fold.

6

Valley folds.

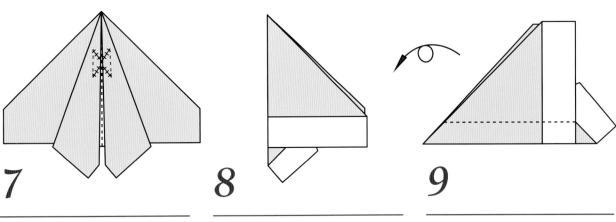

7

Cut front layer, valley fold in half (mountain fold cut flap).

8

Rotate.

9

Valley fold both sides.

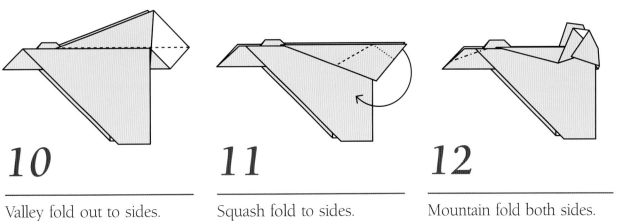

10

Valley fold out to sides.

11

Squash fold to sides.

12

Mountain fold both sides.

Phantom

23

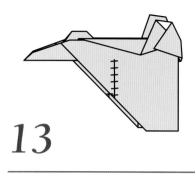

13

Cut as shown, both sides.

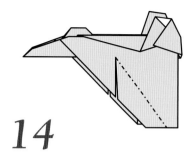

14

Mountain fold both sides.

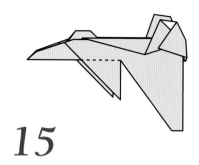

15

Valley folds.

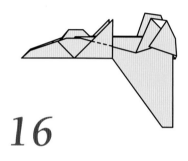

16

Valley fold both sides.

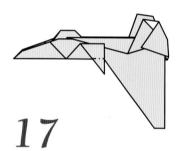

17

Mountain folds both sides, and apply glue to hold.

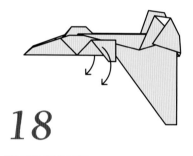

18

Loosen folds to balance.

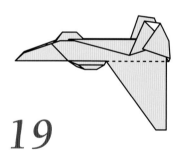

19

Valley fold to balance wings.

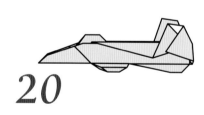

20

Add color.

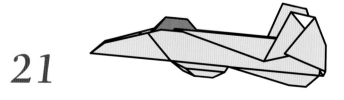

21

Completed Phantom.

Front View

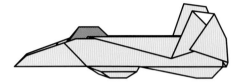

Side View

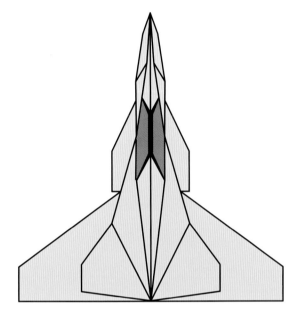

Overhead View

Phantom

B-2 Bomber

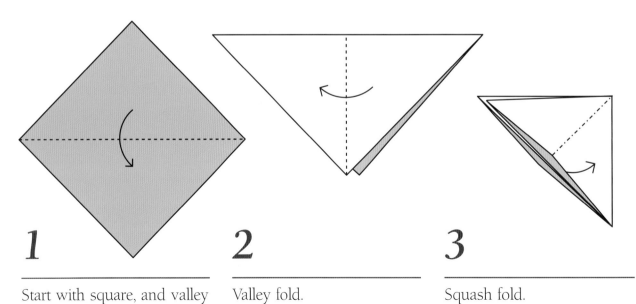

1
Start with square, and valley fold.

2
Valley fold.

3
Squash fold.

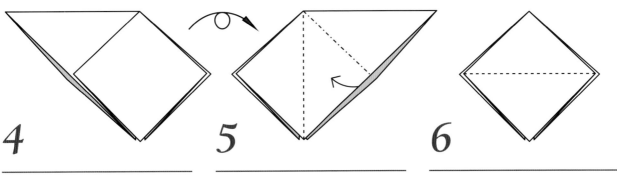

4

Turn over.

5

Squash fold.

6

Valley fold (enlarged follows).

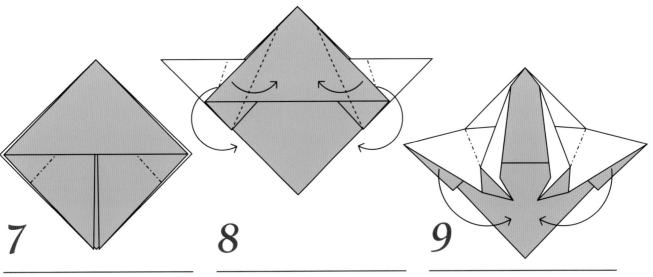

7

Inside reverse fold both sides.

8

Valley and squash fold at same time.

9

Appearance before fold completed.

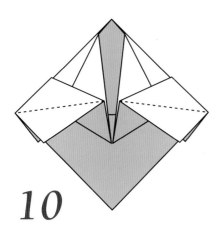

10

Valley folds.

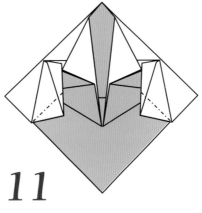

11

Valley folds.

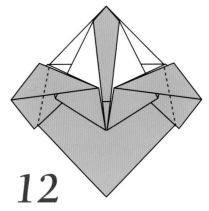

12

Mountain folds.

B-2 Bomber

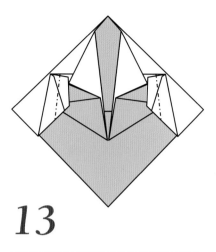

13

Mountain folds.

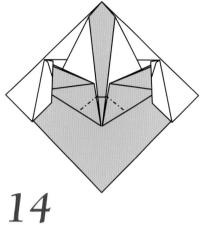

14

Inside reverse folds.

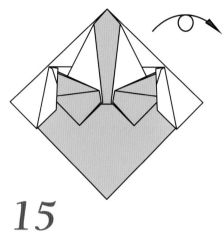

15

Turn over to other side.

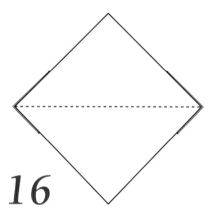

16

Valley fold.

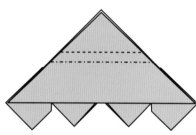

17

Mountain fold, then valley fold.

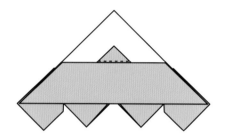

18

Valley fold.

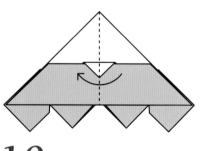

19

Valley fold in half.

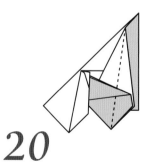

20

Valley fold both sides.

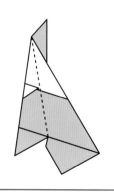

21

Valley fold both sides.

B-2 Bomber

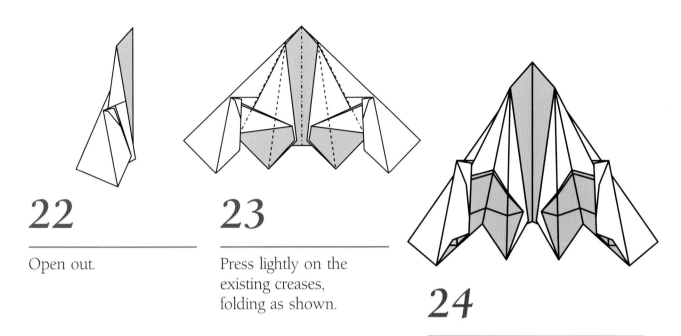

22

Open out.

23

Press lightly on the
existing creases,
folding as shown.

24

Completed B-2 Bomber (overhead view).

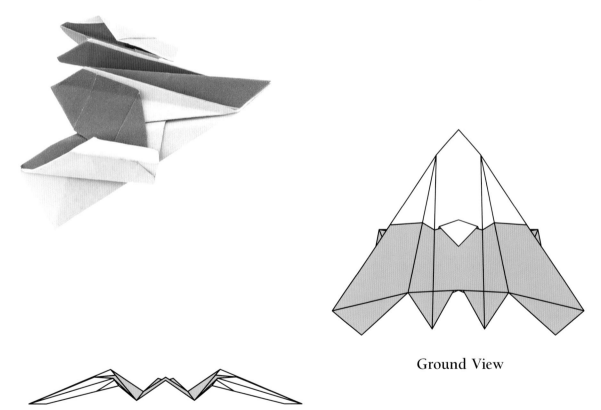

Ground View

Front View

Space Shuttle & Booster

Part 1

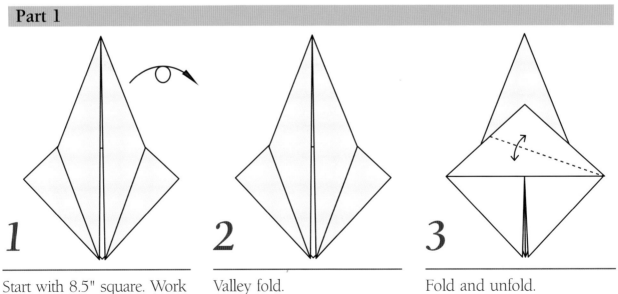

1

Start with 8.5" square. Work Base Fold III to step 11. Turn over.

2

Valley fold.

3

Fold and unfold.

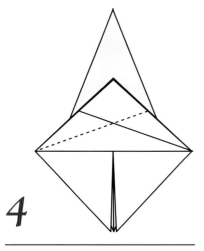

4

Valley fold.

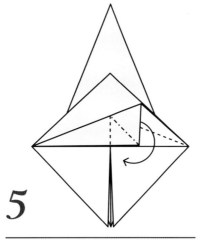

5

Squash fold as shown.

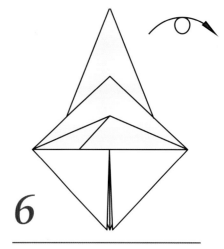

6

Turn over to other side.

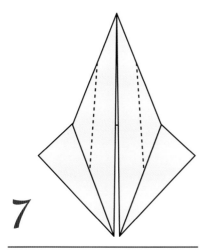

7

Valley folds.

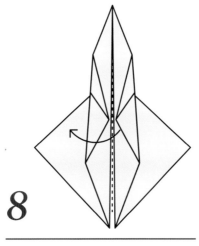

8

Valley fold.

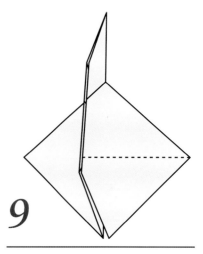

9

Valley fold.

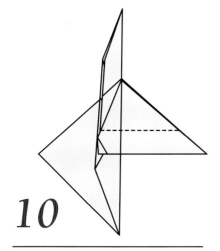

10

Repeat.

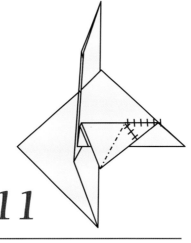

11

Cut and mountain fold.

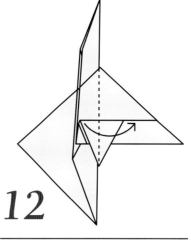

12

Valley fold.

Space Shuttle

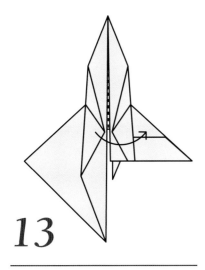

13

Valley fold.

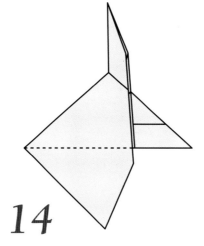

14

Valley fold.

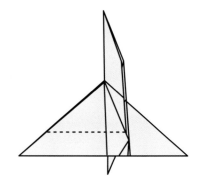

15

Repeat.

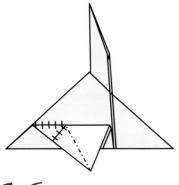

16

Cut and mountain fold.

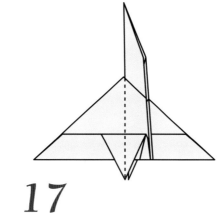

17

Valley fold.

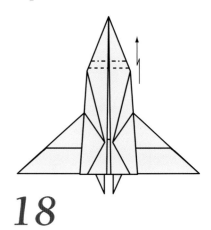

18

Pleat fold.

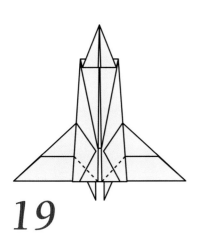

19

Valley folds.

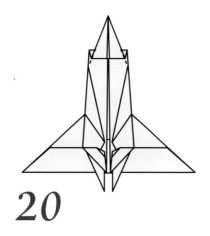

20

Valley folds.

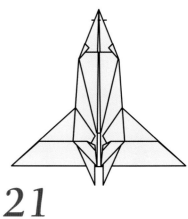

21

Repeat.

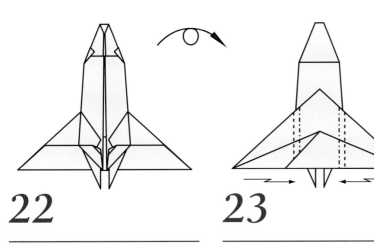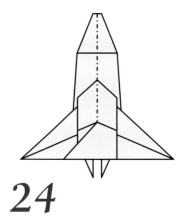

22

Turn over to other side.

23

Pleat folds.

24

Mountain fold in half.

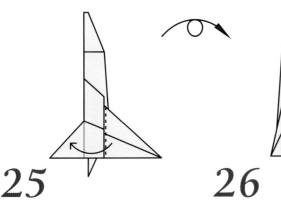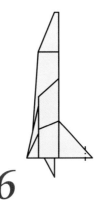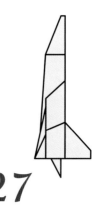

25

Valley fold both sides to balance. Turn over.

26

Inside reverse fold.

27

Add color and detail to tail, see next step.

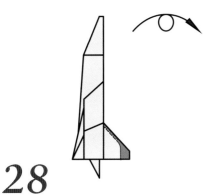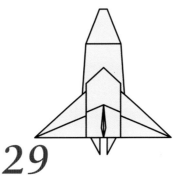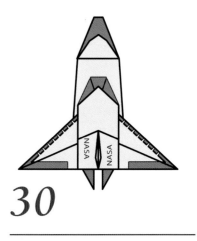

28

Rotate.

29

Add color and detail.

30

Completed part 1 of shuttle.

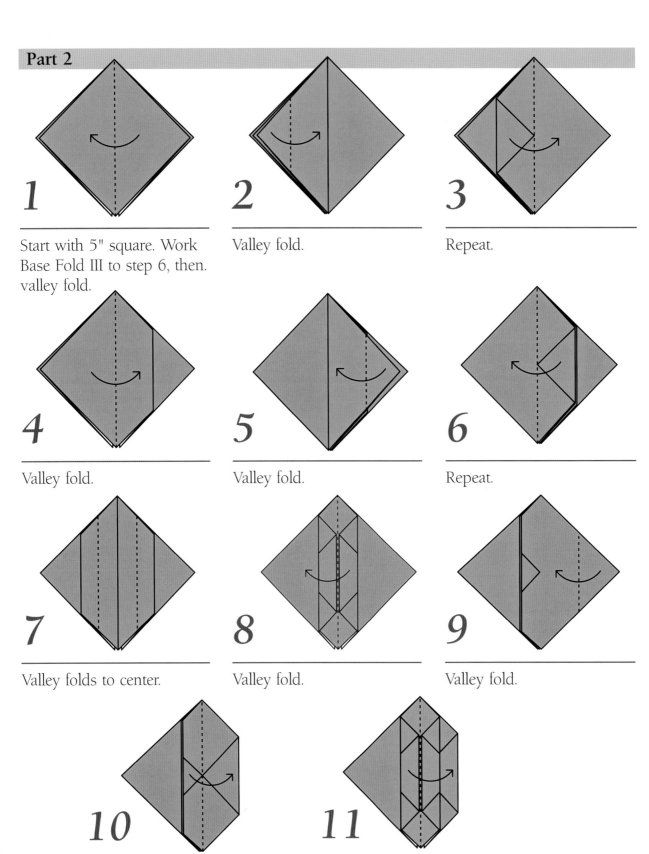

1

Start with 5" square. Work Base Fold III to step 6, then. valley fold.

2

Valley fold.

3

Repeat.

4

Valley fold.

5

Valley fold.

6

Repeat.

7

Valley folds to center.

8

Valley fold.

9

Valley fold.

10

Valley fold.

11

Repeat.

Space Shuttle

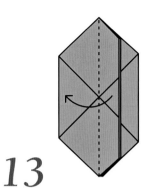

12

Valley fold.

13

Valley fold.

14

Completed part 2 of shuttle.

Part 3

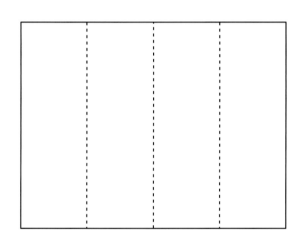

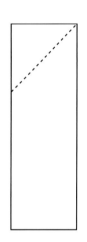

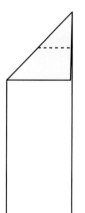

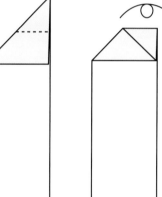

1

Start with full sheet of paper (8.5" by 11").

2

Valley fold.

3

Repeat.

4

Unfold and rotate.

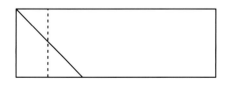

5

Valley fold.

6

Inside reverse folds.

Space Shuttle

35

7

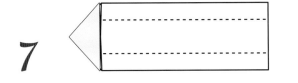

Valley folds.

8

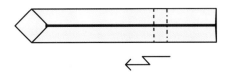

Pleat fold.

9

Squash folds.

10

Add detail.

11

Valley fold in half.

12

Add detail.

13

Completed part 3 (booster rocket).

Note: Make second booster rocket for shuttle.

To Attach

1

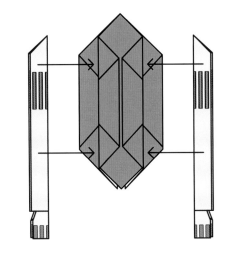

Join part 2 and the two part 3 boosters, and apply glue to hold.

2

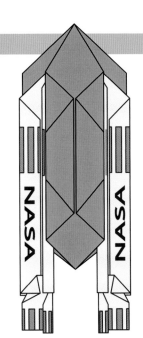

Completed shuttle booster.

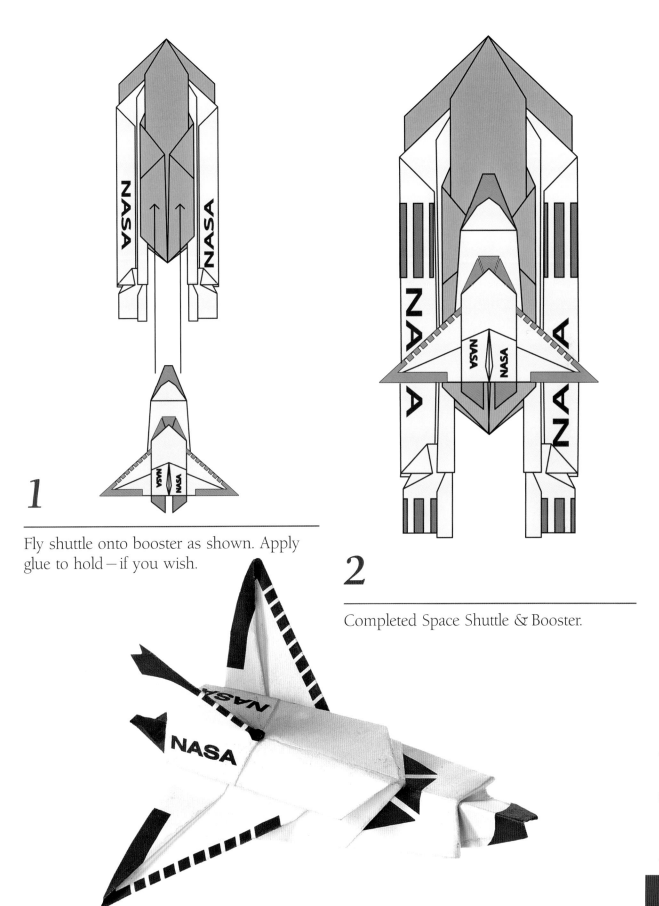

1

Fly shuttle onto booster as shown. Apply glue to hold – if you wish.

2

Completed Space Shuttle & Booster.

Apache Helicopter

---Part 1

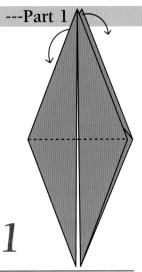

1

Start with Base Fold III. Valley fold both sides.

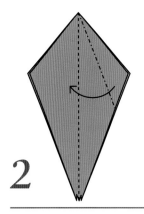

2

Valley fold and squash fold.

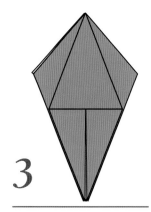

3

Turn over to other side.

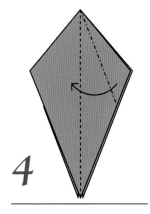

4

Repeat step 2.

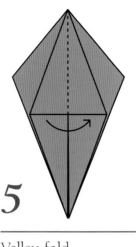

5

Valley fold.

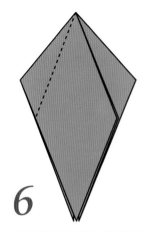

6

Valley fold.

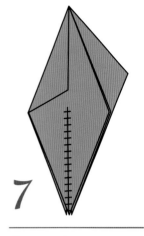

7

Cut as shown.

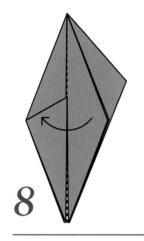

8

Valley fold.

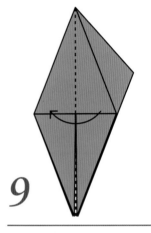

9

Valley fold.

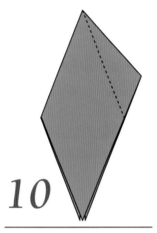

10

Valley fold.

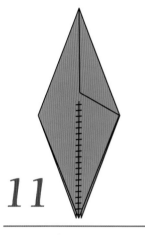

11

Cut as shown.

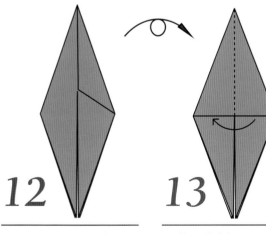

12

Turn over to other side.

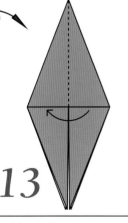

13

Valley fold.

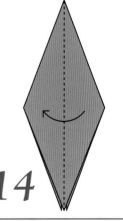

14

Valley fold.

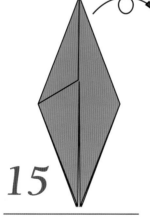

15

Turn over to other side.

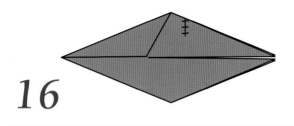

16

Cut as shown through all layers.

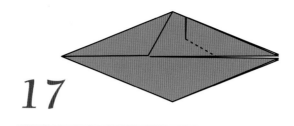

17

Valley fold both sides.

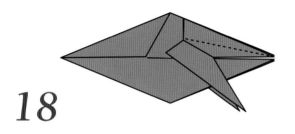

18

Valley fold both front and back.

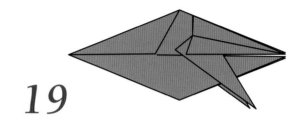

19

Tuck fold beneath lower flap.

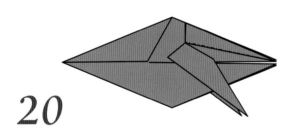

20

Mountain fold both sides to center.

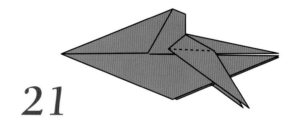

21

Valley fold both front and back.

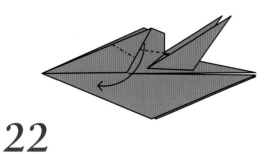

22

Inside reverse fold both sides.

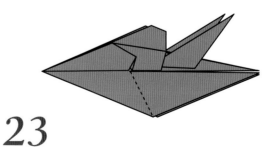

23

Valley fold both front and back.

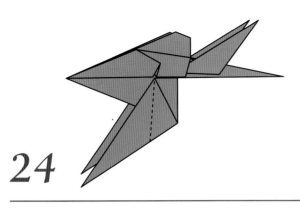

24

Valley fold both sides.

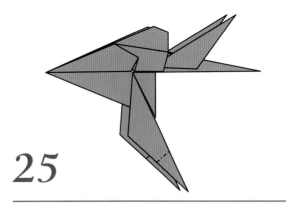

25

Inside reverse fold both sides.

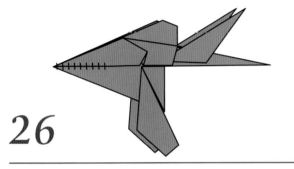

26

Cut as shown.

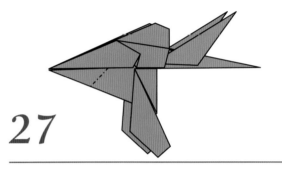

27

Inside reverse fold.

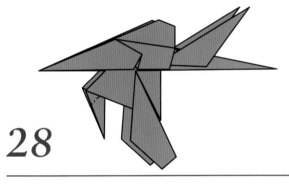

28

Repeat inside reverse fold.

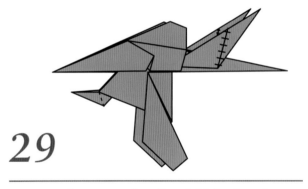

29

Cuts as shown and valley fold both sides.

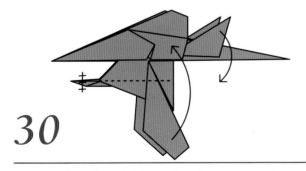

30

Cut, and valley folds to level wings and tail flaps.

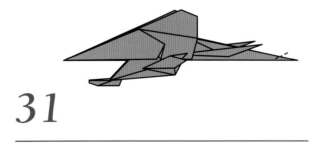

31

Inside reverse fold both sides.

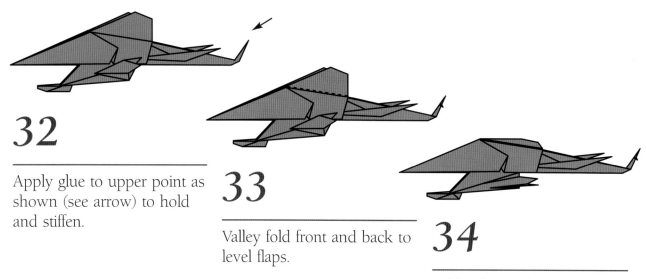

32

Apply glue to upper point as shown (see arrow) to hold and stiffen.

33

Valley fold front and back to level flaps.

34

Add color or detail.

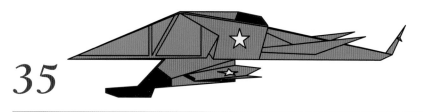

35

Completed part 1 of helicopter.

Part 2

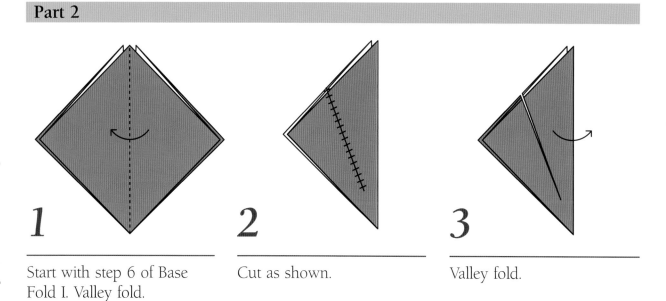

1

Start with step 6 of Base Fold I. Valley fold.

2

Cut as shown.

3

Valley fold.

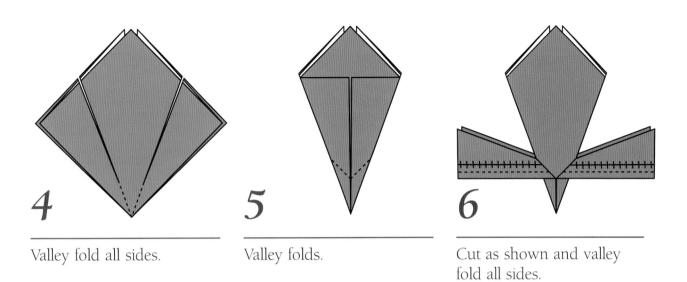

4

Valley fold all sides.

5

Valley folds.

6

Cut as shown and valley fold all sides.

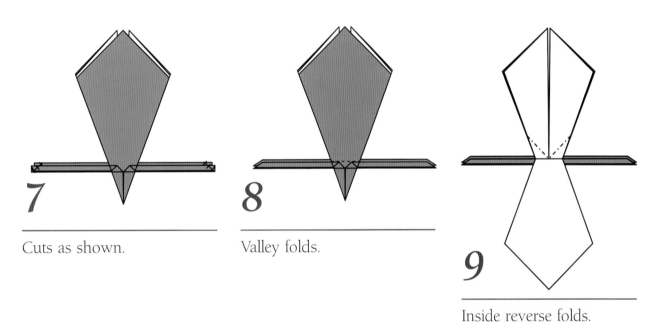

7

Cuts as shown.

8

Valley folds.

9

Inside reverse folds.

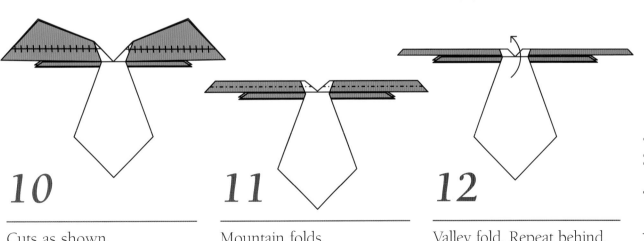

10

Cuts as shown.

11

Mountain folds.

12

Valley fold. Repeat behind.

Apache Helicopter

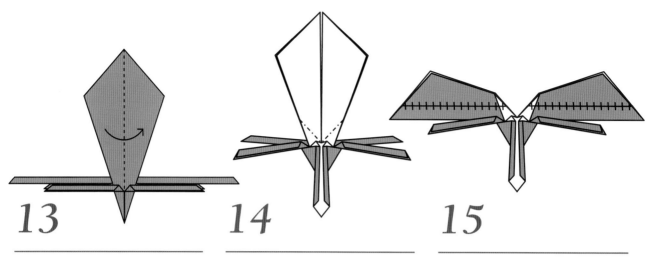

13

Valley folds both front and back.

14

Inside reverse folds.

15

Cuts as shown.

Note: Make a second, smaller-size propeller for tail rotor.

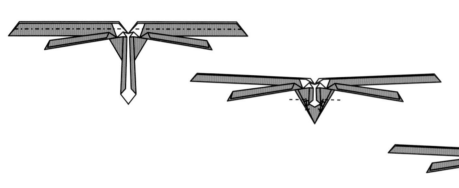

16

Mountain folds.

17

Cuts, valley folds, and open all four sides.

18

Completed part 2 of helicopter.

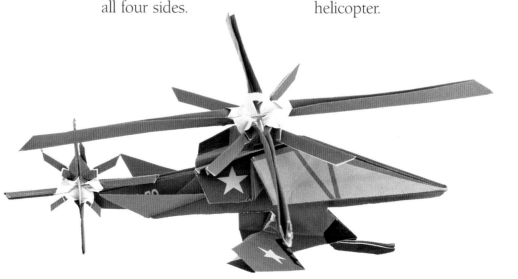

1

Apply glue to outer part of a small tube (or roll a section of paper into a small tube). Insert tube into top of helicopter as shown and let dry. This will allow propeller to turn.

Join parts together. Glue tail rotor onto tail to hold.

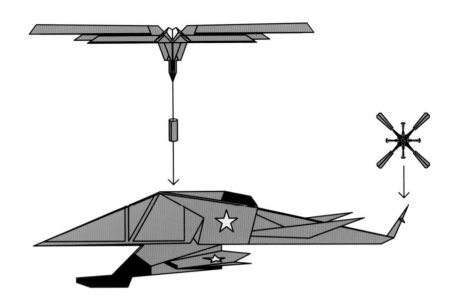

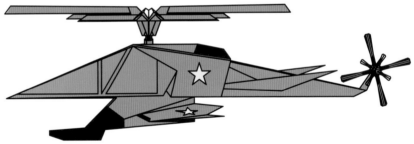

2

Completed Apache Helicopter.

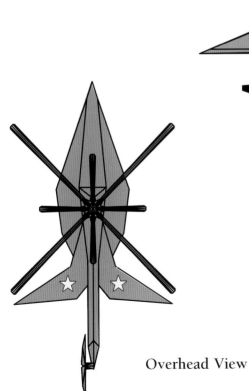

Overhead View

Side-Panel Truck

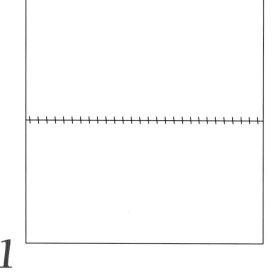

1

Cut an origami square in half.

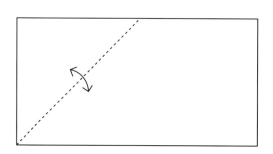

2

Valley fold to edge, then unfold.

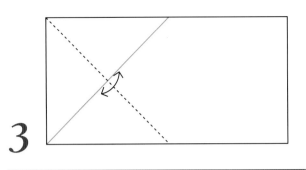

3

Repeat at other angle.

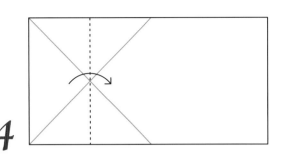

4

Valley fold where creases cross.

5

Inside reverse folds.

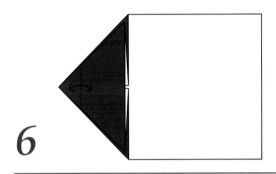

6

Valley fold then unfold.

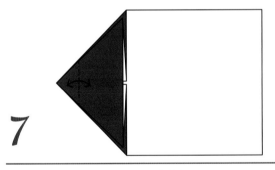

7

Mountain fold then unfold.

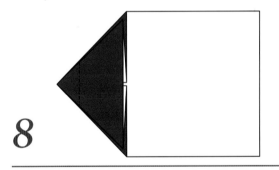

8

Mountain fold front and back to sink.

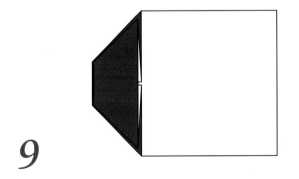

9

Turn over to other side.

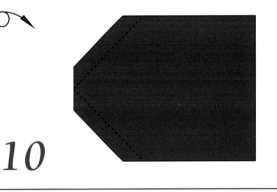

10

Valley folds.

Side-Panel Truck

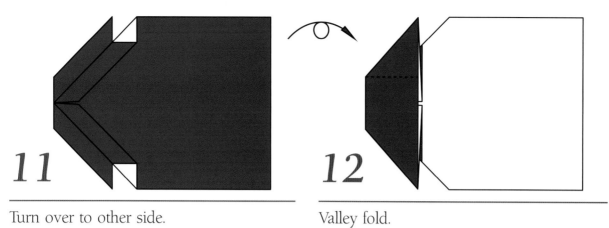

11

Turn over to other side.

12

Valley fold.

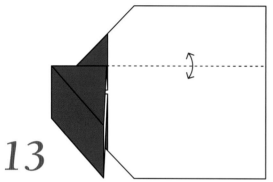

13

Valley fold then unfold.

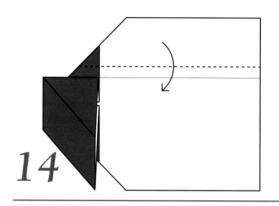

14

Valley fold.

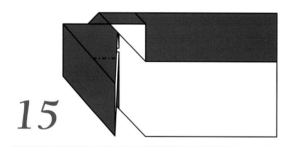

15

Mountain fold.

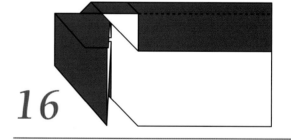

16

Valley fold.

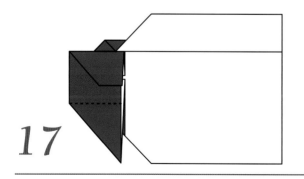

17

Valley fold.

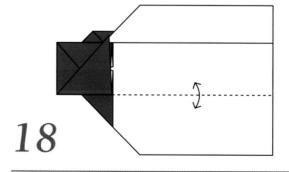

18

Valley fold then unfold.

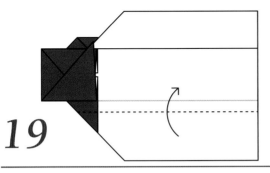

19

Valley fold.

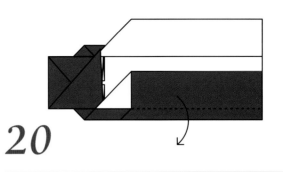

20

Valley fold.

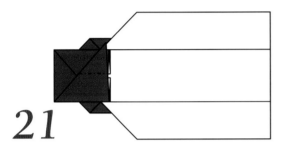

21

Mountain fold.

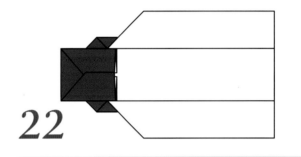

22

Unfold.

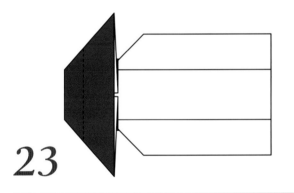

23

Valley fold.

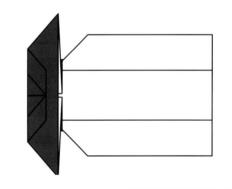

24

Unfold.

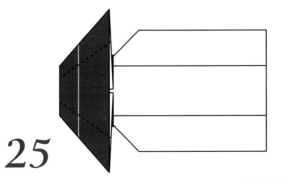

25

Valley folds.

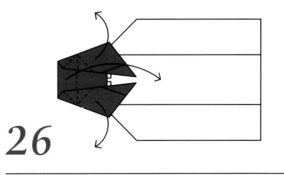

26

Inside reverse folds, opening sides to form boxlike shape at same time.

Side-Panel Truck

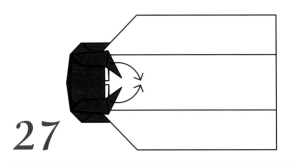

27

Appearance before completed.

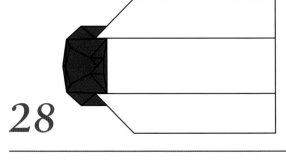

28

Apply glue to hold cab in position.

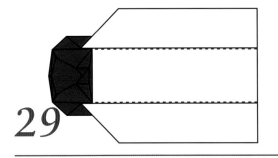

29

Unvalley side flaps to vertical position.

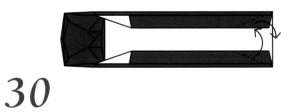

30

Mountain fold both tips together and apply glue to hold.

31

Completed truck body.

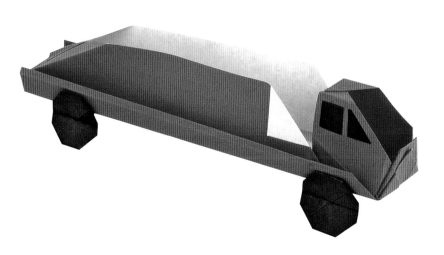

Wheels (all road vehicles)

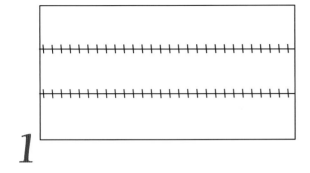

1

Cut remaining half square into three equal strips.

2

Valley fold.

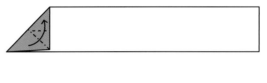

3

Squash fold.

4

Valley fold then unfold to crease. Distance of crease indicated should be width of vehicle.

5

Valley fold.

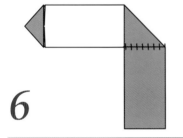

6

Cut as shown.

7

Squash fold.

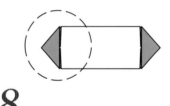

8

See close-ups for detail.

9

Valley fold, then unfold.

10

Unfold.

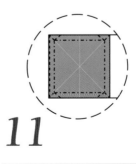

11

Mountain folds (valley corners).

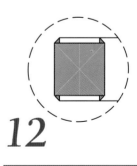

12

Return to full view.

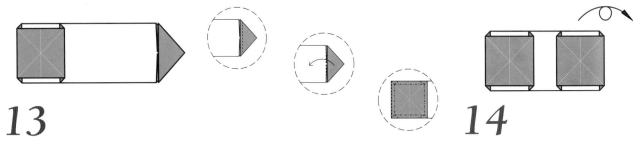

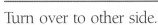

13

Repeat steps on other end.

14

Turn over to other side.

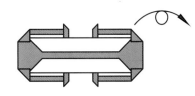

15

Valley folds.

16

Valley folds.

17

Turn over to other side.

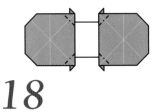

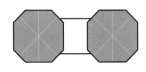

18

Mountain folds.

19

Turn over to other side.

20

Valley folds.

21

Completed sets of wheels. You'll need 2 sets to complete this side-panel truck—3 sets for a 6-wheeler.

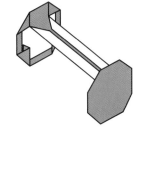

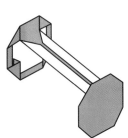

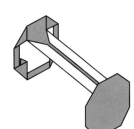

To Attach

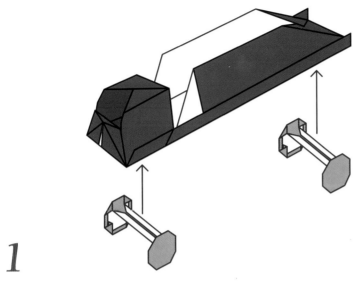

1

Join all parts together as shown and apply glue to hold.

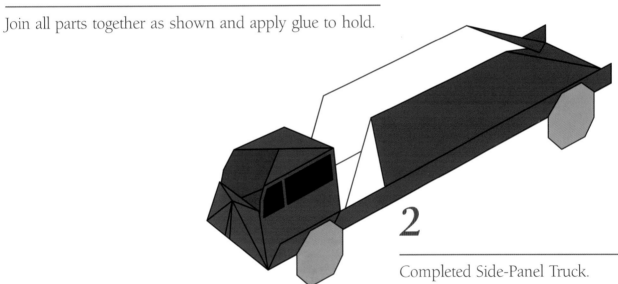

2

Completed Side-Panel Truck.

Note: Add another set of wheels as shown for a heavy-duty 6-wheeler.

Side-Panel Truck

Container Truck

Part 1

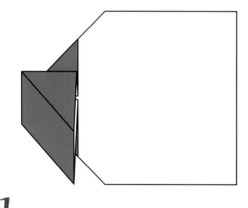

1

Work through to step 13 of the Side-Panel Truck (see pages 46–48). Valley fold.

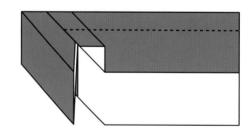

2

Valley fold.

3

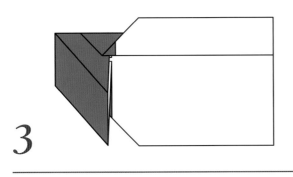

Tuck flap behind end layer.

4

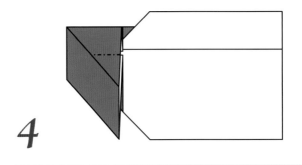

Mountain fold.

5

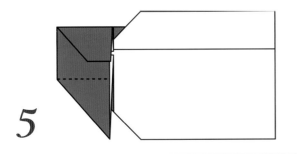

Valley fold.

6

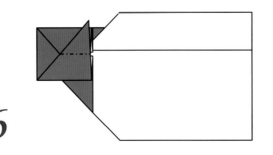

Mountain fold.

7

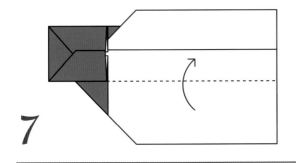

Valley fold in direction of arrow.

8

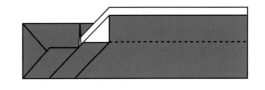

Valley fold.

9

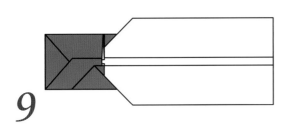

Tuck flap behind end layer.

10

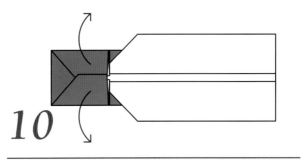

Unfold outward as shown.

Container Truck

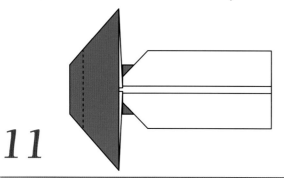

11

Valley fold, then unfold.

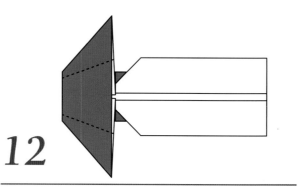

12

Valley folds.

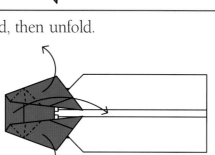

13

Inside reverse folds, opening sides to form boxlike shape.

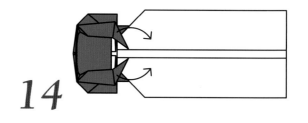

14

Appearance before completion.

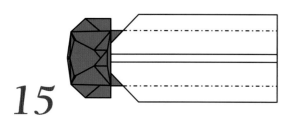

15

Apply glue to tips. Mountain folds. Rotate.

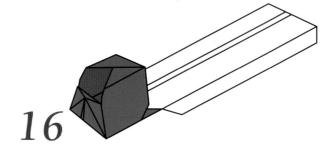

16

Completed part 1 of container truck.

Part 2

1

Start with full sheet of paper (8.5" by 11"). Mountain folds.

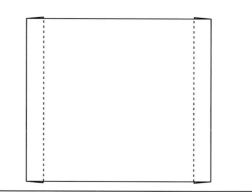

2

Valley folds.

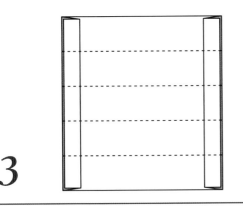

3

Valley folds, tucking sides into each other.

4

Appearance before completion.

5

Rotate to front.

 6

Valley fold.

 7

Repeat.

 8

Valley fold.

 9

Repeat.

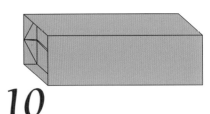 **10**

Completed part 2 of container truck.

To Attach

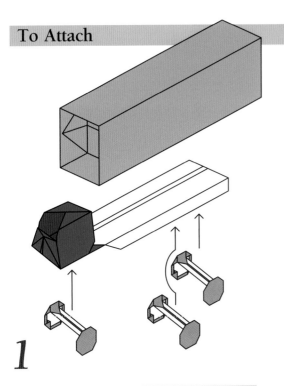

1

Join all parts together as shown and apply glue to hold.

Note: Make 3 sets of wheels (to match width of truck). See pages 51–52.

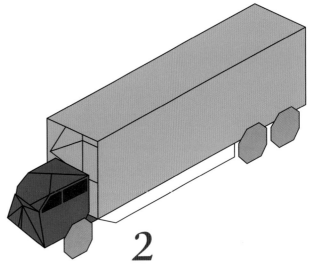

2

Completed Container Truck.

Car

Part 1

1

Start with 4" by 10" paper and valley fold both ends.

2

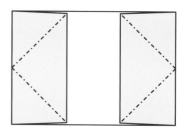

Inside reverse folds.

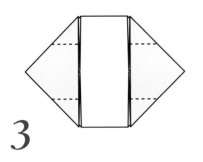

3

Valley fold and glue.

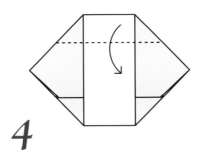

4

Valley folds.

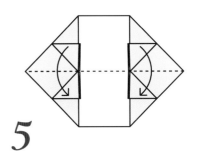

5

Valley fold and glue.

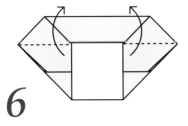

6

Valley folds and glue.

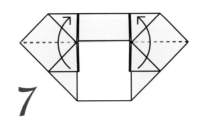

7

Valley fold.

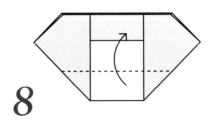

8

Valley fold and glue.

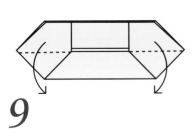

9

Valley fold.

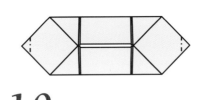

10

Mountain fold ends to sink, pushing inward.

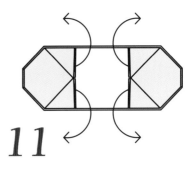

11

Pull to open as indicated.

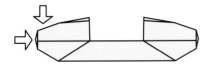

12

Push down and in to fold, lowering front end of car.

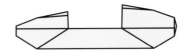

13

Completed part 1 of car.

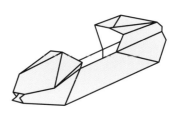

Angled View

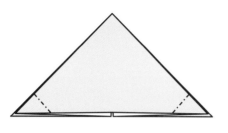

1

Start with Base Fold II, using 3" square.

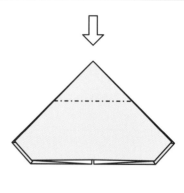

2

Push down, mountain folding all around as indicated to open all sides.

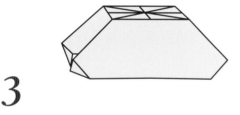

3

Add color and detail to completion.

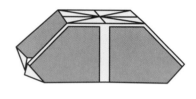

4

Completed part 2 (cab) of car.

Note: Make two sets of wheels for your car. Instructions on pages 51–52.

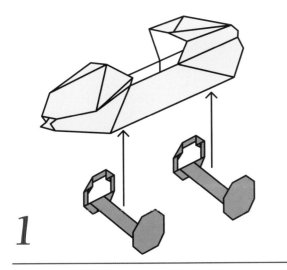

1

Add wheels and apply glue to hold.

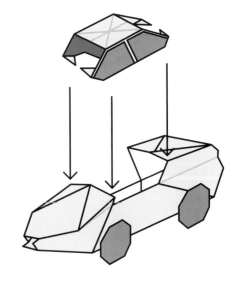

2

Position cab section into place and apply glue to hold.

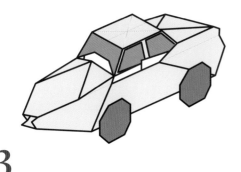

3

Completed Car.

Front View

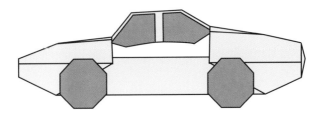

Side View

Minivan and Trailer

Part 1

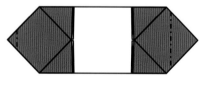

1

Start with step 11 of the Car (page 59). Push ends inward and mountain fold to sink.

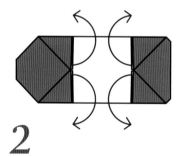

2

Pull in direction of arrows to open sides. Rotate.

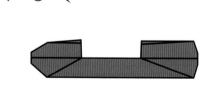

3

Completed part 1 of minivan.

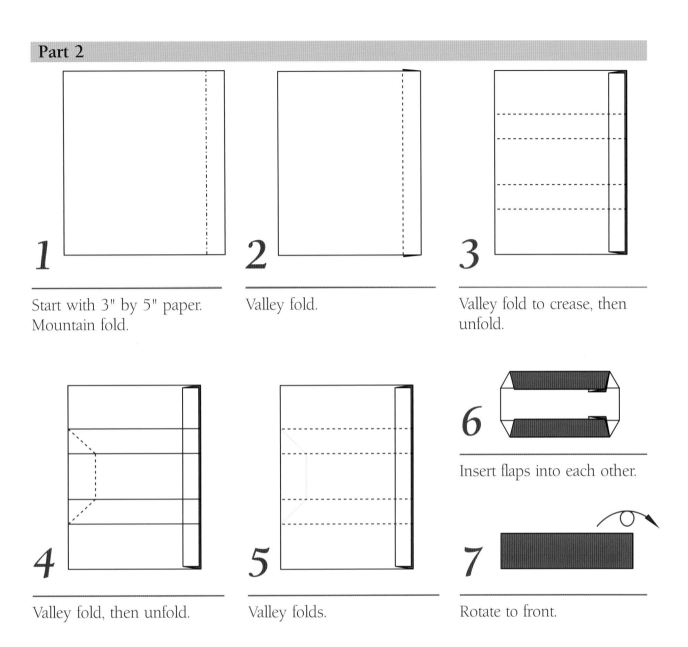

1 Start with 3" by 5" paper. Mountain fold.

2 Valley fold.

3 Valley fold to crease, then unfold.

4 Valley fold, then unfold.

5 Valley folds.

6 Insert flaps into each other.

7 Rotate to front.

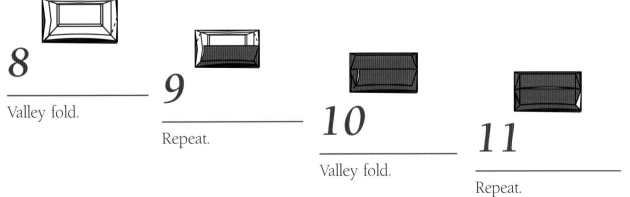

8 Valley fold.

9 Repeat.

10 Valley fold.

11 Repeat.

Minivan

63

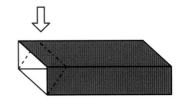

12

Push and fold. Add color.

13

Add detail and windows.

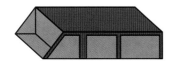

14

Completed part 2 of minivan.

Note: Make two sets of wheels for your minivan. Instructions on pages 51–52.

To Attach

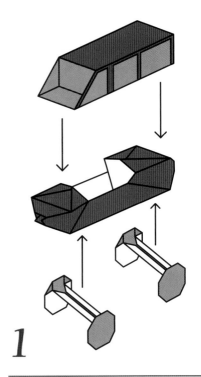

1

Join all parts together as shown and apply glue to hold.

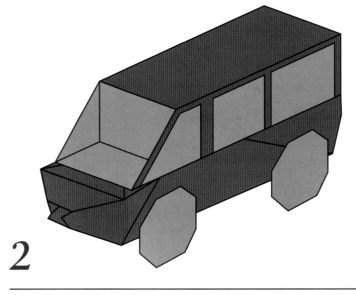

2

Completed Minivan.

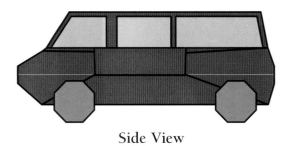

Side View

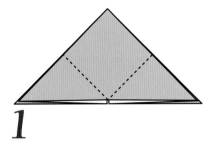

1

Start with Base Fold II and valley fold.

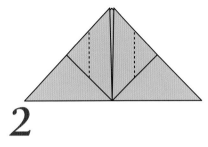

2

Valley folds.

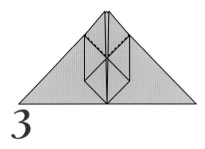

3

Valley folds.

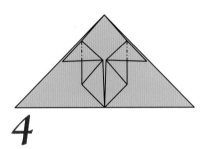

4

Mountain folds.

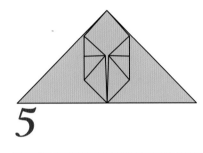

5

Unfolds.

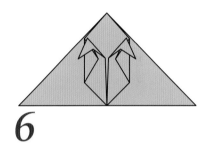

6

Place tips into openings to lock.

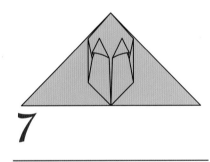

7

Appearance before completion.

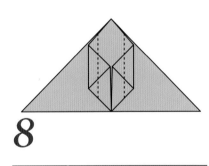

8

Valley folds and glue to hold.

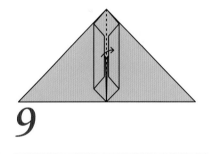

9

Valley fold as shown.

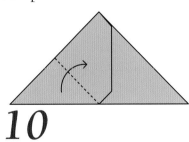

10

Valley fold.

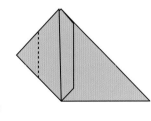

11

Valley fold.

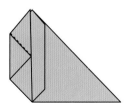

12

Valley fold.

Minivan

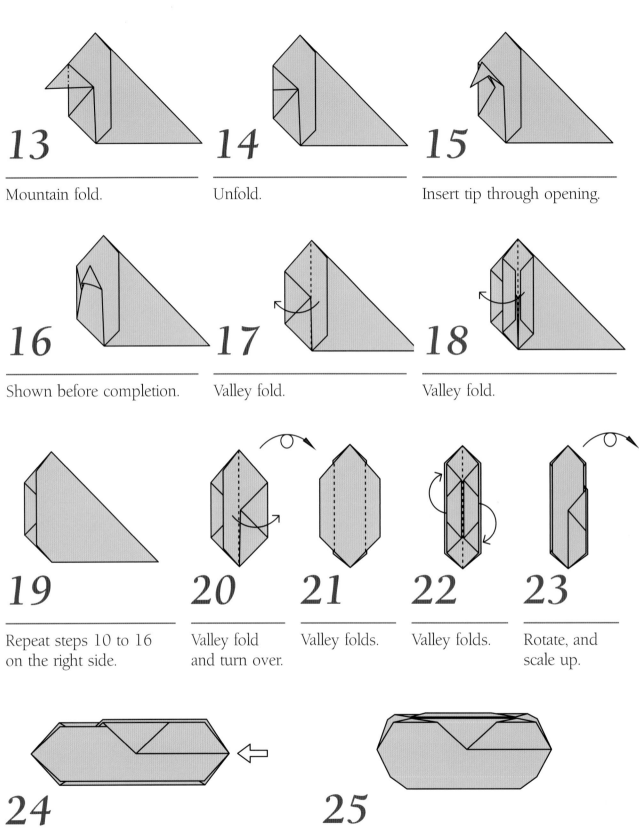

13

Mountain fold.

14

Unfold.

15

Insert tip through opening.

16

Shown before completion.

17

Valley fold.

18

Valley fold.

19

Repeat steps 10 to 16 on the right side.

20

Valley fold and turn over.

21

Valley folds.

22

Valley folds.

23

Rotate, and scale up.

24

Blow into opening at end to inflate.

25

Completed trailer compartment.

Make a single set of wheels
(see pages 51-52) for the trailer.

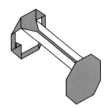

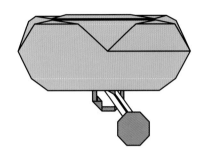

1

Attach the set of wheels towards the
rear of the trailer, glue to hold.

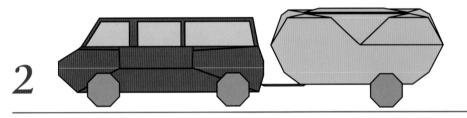

2

Fold a small section of paper into a thin strip to join minivan and
trailer together, glue to hold.

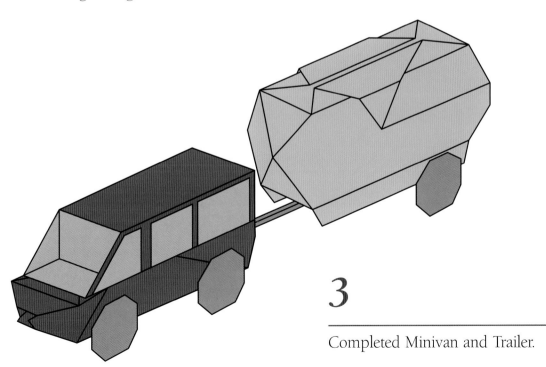

3

Completed Minivan and Trailer.

Minivan

Snowmobile with Trailer

Part 1

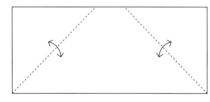

1

Start with rectangular sheet of paper (3" by 6.5"). Valley fold and unfold.

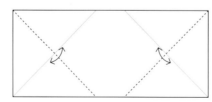

2

Valley folds then unfold.

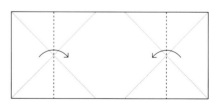

3

Valley folds.

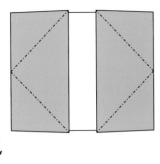

4

Inside reverse folds.

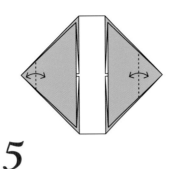

5

Valley folds then unfold.

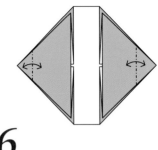

6

Mountain folds then unfold.

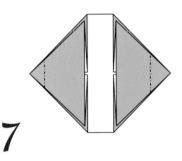

7

Push in and fold to sink.

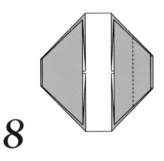

8

Valley fold.

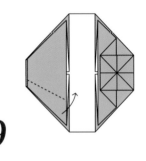

9

Valley fold.

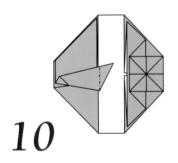

10

Mountain fold.

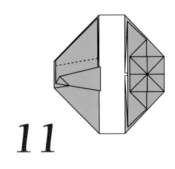

11

Valley fold.

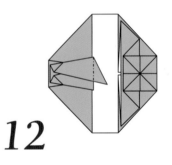

12

Mountain fold.

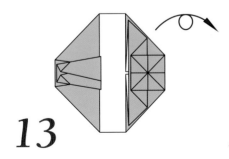

13

Turn over to other side.

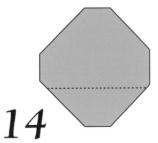

14

Valley fold.

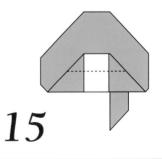

15

Valley fold.

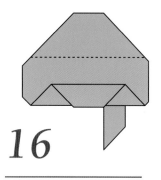

16

Valley fold.

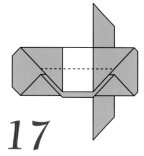

17

Valley fold.

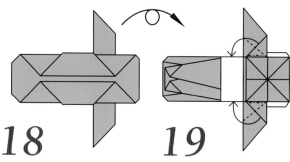

18

Turn over to other side.

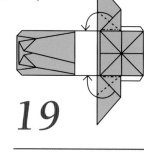

19

Squash folds.

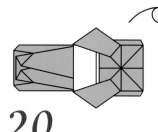

20

Rotate to side view.

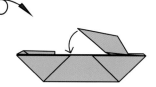

21

Pull and apply glue to hold.

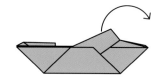

22

Pull and fold.

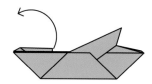

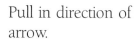

23

Pull in direction of arrow.

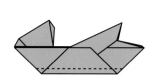

24

Valley folds.

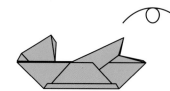

25

Rotate to rear view.

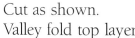

26

Cut as shown.
Valley fold top layer.

27

Valley fold back layer.

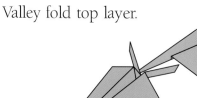

28

Completed Snowmobile.

1

Start with a rectangular sheet of paper (3" by 7"). Valley fold then unfold.

2

Mountain folds.

3

Valley fold.

4

Valley fold.

5

Valley fold.

6

Valley fold.

7

Mountain folds.

8

Mountain fold, then unfold to step 7.

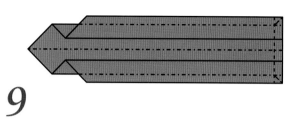

9

Mountain folds and inside reverse folds at corners.

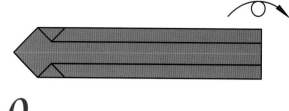

10

Apply glue to hold. Rotate to side view.

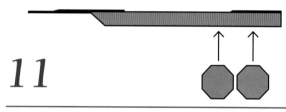

11

Make and add two sets of wheels toward rear of trailer, glue to hold.

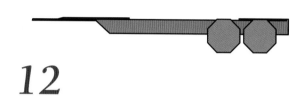

12

Completed trailer.

To Attach

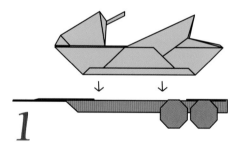

1

Position snowmobile onto trailer. If you wish, apply glue to hold.

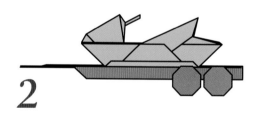

2

Completed Snowmobile with Trailer.

3

Attach the trailer to a car, van, or an SUV (minivan cab and car body combo), and you're ready to go!

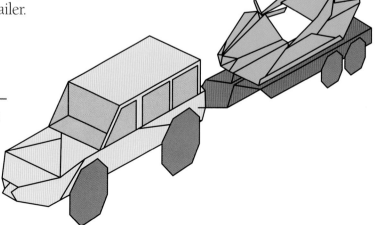

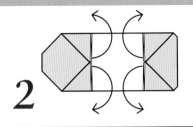
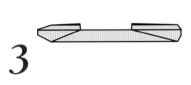

1

Work steps 1 through 10 of Car (pages 58–59). At step 11, push inward and sink.

2

Pull in direction of arrows, opening all sides. Rotate.

3

Completed chassis.

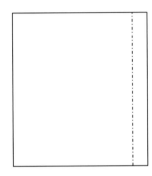
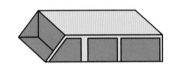

4

Fold new 3" by 5" paper in matching color. Follow Minivan part 2 steps (pages 63–64).

5

Completed cab.

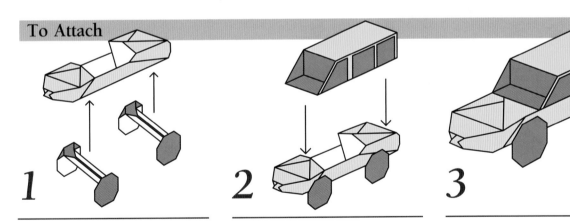

1

Attach wheels to chassis.

2

Position cab and glue to hold.

3

Completed SUV.

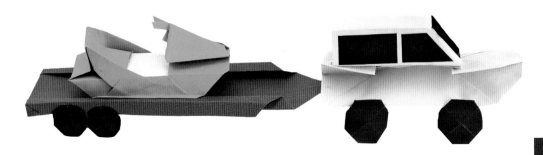

Snowmobile

Submarine

Part 1

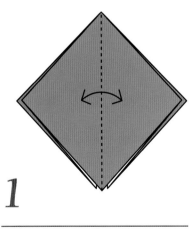

1

Start at step 6 of Base Fold III. Valley and unfold.

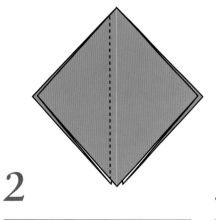

2

Valley fold.

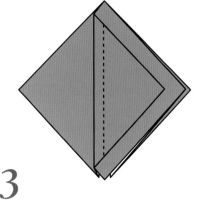

3

Valley fold.

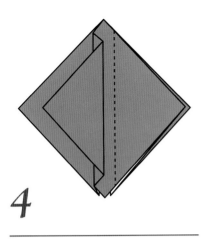

4

Valley fold.

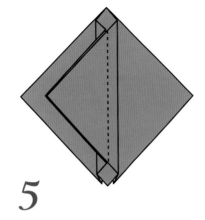

5

Valley fold.

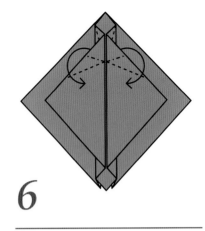

6

Valley and squash folds.

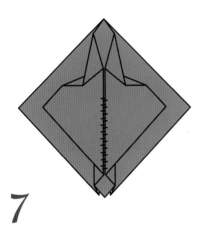

7

Make cuts as shown.

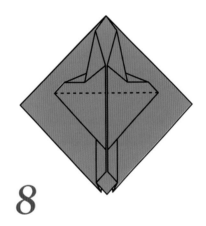

8

Valley folds.

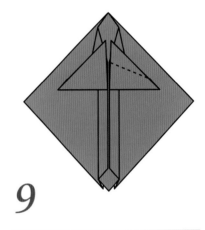

9

Valley fold.

10

Mountain fold. Bring back layer to front.

11

Repeat steps 9 and 10 on left side.

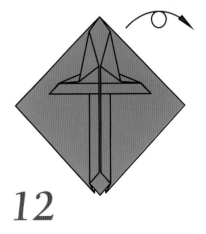

12

Turn over to other side.

Submarine

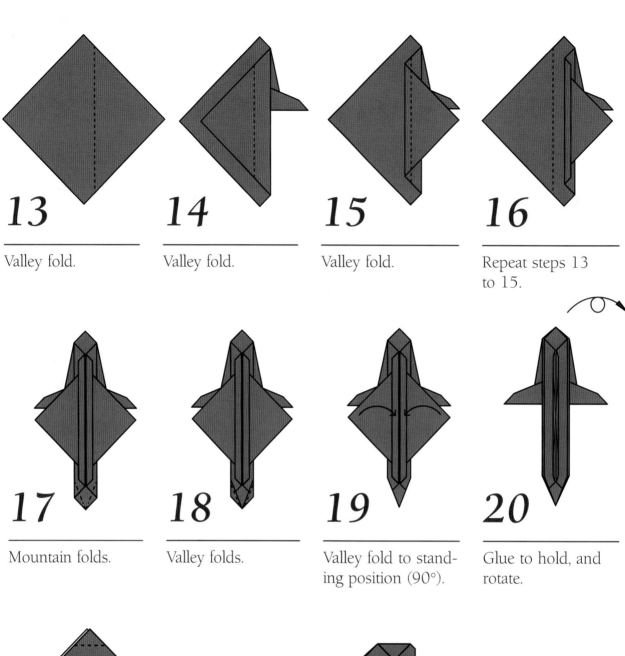

13
Valley fold.

14
Valley fold.

15
Valley fold.

16
Repeat steps 13 to 15.

17
Mountain folds.

18
Valley folds.

19
Valley fold to standing position (90°).

20
Glue to hold, and rotate.

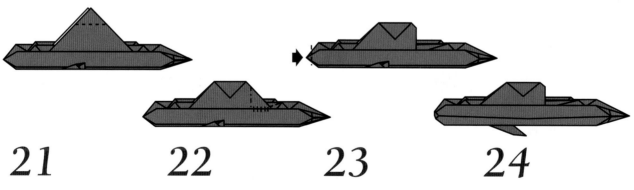

21
Valley fold layers together and glue.

22
Cut and mountain fold cut parts.

23
Push inward, opening sub out slightly.

24
Completed part 1 of submarine.

Part 2

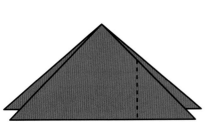

1

Start with Base Fold II and valley fold.

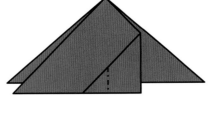

2

Mountain fold.

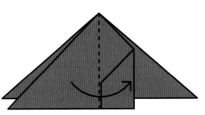

3

Valley fold.

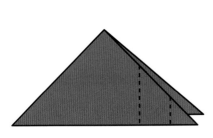

4

Repeat steps 1 and 2.

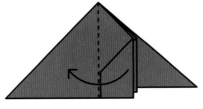

5

Valley fold.

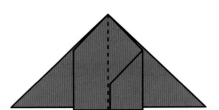

6

Valley fold.

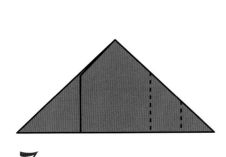

7

Repeat steps 1 and 2.

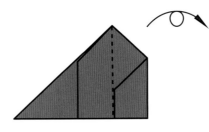

8

Valley fold and turn over..

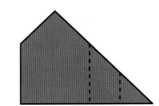

9

Repeat steps 1 and 2.

Submarine

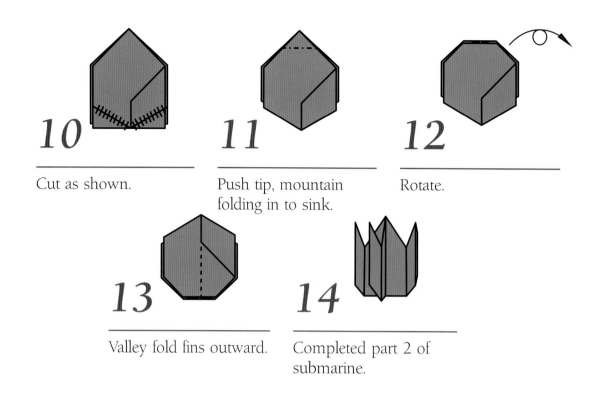

10 Cut as shown.

11 Push tip, mountain folding in to sink.

12 Rotate.

13 Valley fold fins outward.

14 Completed part 2 of submarine.

To Attach

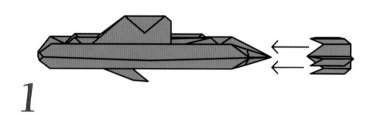

1 Insert end of part 1 into part 2 as shown. Apply glue to hold.

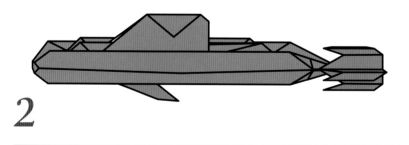

2 Completed Submarine.

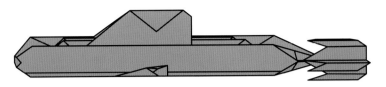

Side View

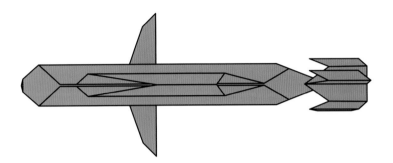

Overhead View

Submarine

79

Spanish Galleon

Part 1

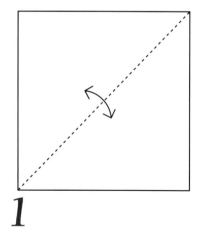

1

Start with 8.5" square.
Valley fold then unfold.

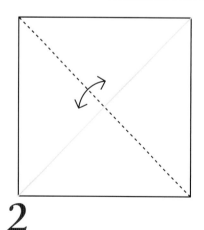

2

Valley fold then unfold.

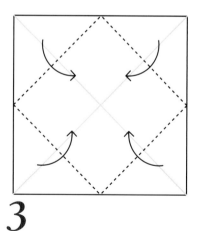

3

Valley folds to center.

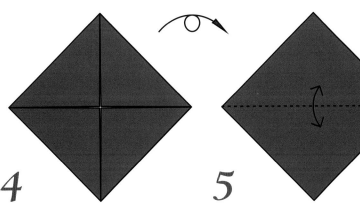
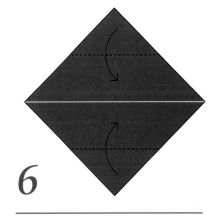

4

Turn over to other side.

5

Valley fold then unfold.

6

Valley folds.

7

Mountain fold.

8

Outside reverse folds.

9

Unfold to step 7.

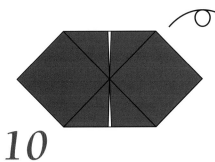
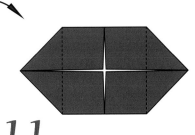

10

Turn over to other side.

11

Valley folds.

12

Valley fold.

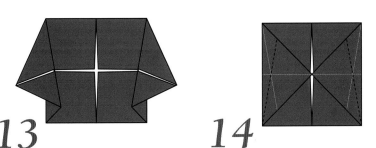
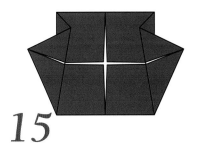

13

Unfold.

14

Valley fold.

15

Unfold.

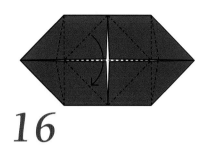

16

Fold as marked, pushing center inward at same time.

17

Appearance of folds before completion.

18

Pull some paper outward on both front and back.

19

Mountain fold both sides.

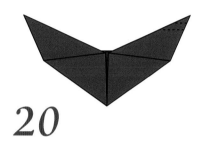

20

Outside reverse, then repeat.

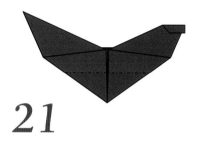

21

Mountain fold both sides.

22

Inside reverse fold. Rotate to top view.

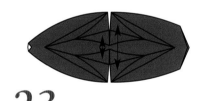

23

Glue sections together on each side as shown.

24

Punch 3 holes into form, as shown by circles, for masts.

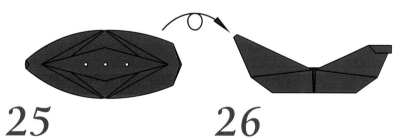
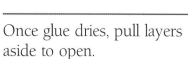

25

Rotate to side view.

26

Once glue dries, pull layers aside to open.

27

Completed part 1 of Spanish galleon.

Part 2

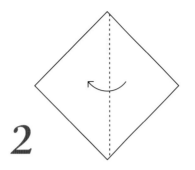

1
Start with 4.25" square.
Valley fold and unfold.

2
Valley fold near crease.

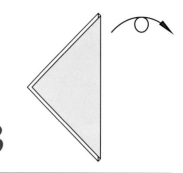

3
Turn over to other side.

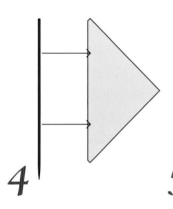

4
Add stick or tightly
rolled paper, and
apply glue.

5
Pleat fold layers
around mast to hold.

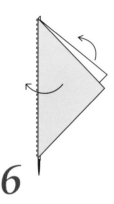

6
Valley fold.

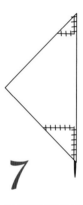

7
Cut as shown,
through both layers.

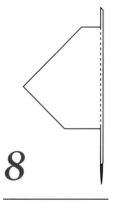

8
Valley folds.
front and back

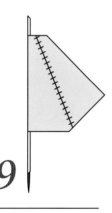

9
Cut as shown.

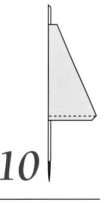

10
Valley folds
both sides.

11
Unfold.

12
Completed part
2 of Spanish
galleon.

Spanish Galleon

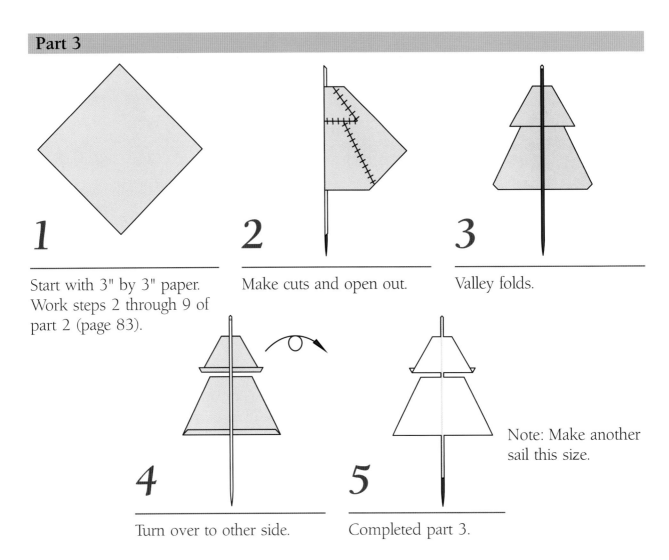

Part 3

1

Start with 3" by 3" paper. Work steps 2 through 9 of part 2 (page 83).

2

Make cuts and open out.

3

Valley folds.

4

Turn over to other side.

5

Completed part 3.

Note: Make another sail this size.

Part 4

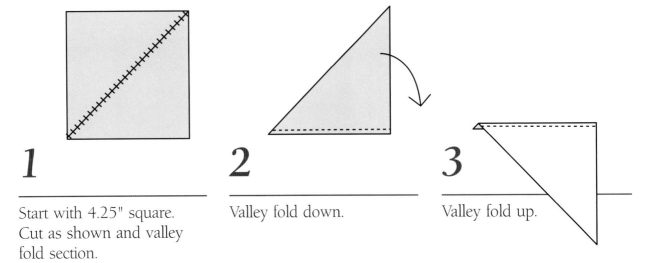

1

Start with 4.25" square. Cut as shown and valley fold section.

2

Valley fold down.

3

Valley fold up.

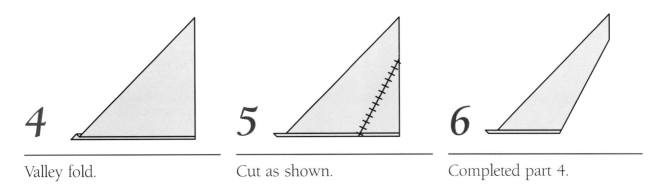

4 Valley fold.

5 Cut as shown.

6 Completed part 4.

To Attach

1

Place 3 sails with masts (parts 2 and 3) into holes in part 1 as shown and apply glue to hold. Glue bowsprit sail (part 4) to front of ship and to first mast.

2

Completed Spanish Galleon.

Spanish Galleon

Aircraft Carrier

Part 1

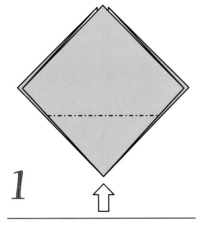

1

Start at step 6 of Base Fold III. Invert. Mountain fold front and back to sink tip.

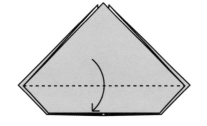

2

Valley fold.

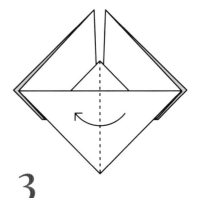

3

Valley fold.

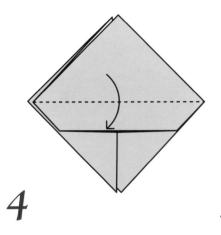

4

Valley fold.

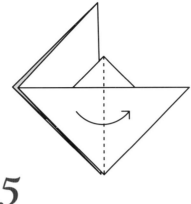

5

Valley fold.

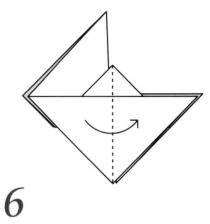

6

Repeat.

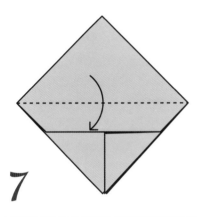

7

Valley fold.

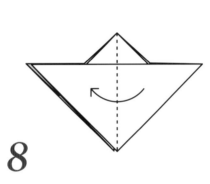

8

Valley fold.

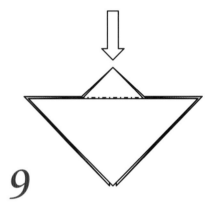

9

Push tip downward to sink, mountain folding front and back.

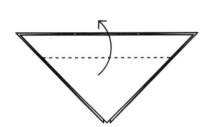

10

Valley fold both sides.

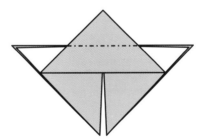

11

Mountain fold tips to inside, front and back.

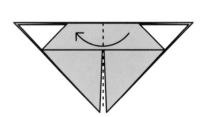

12

Valley fold.

Aircraft Carrier

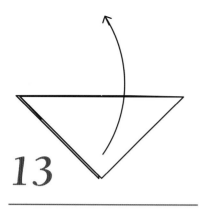

13

Valley fold.

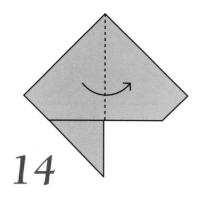

14

Valley fold.

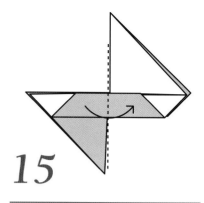

15

Valley fold.

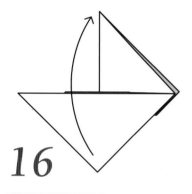

16

Valley fold.

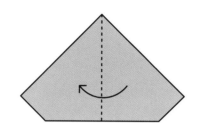

17

Valley fold.

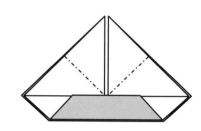

18

Inside reverse folds.

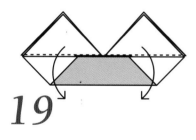

19

Valley fold both sides.

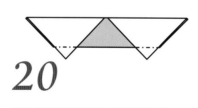

20

Mountain folds and glue.

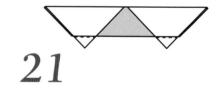

21

Valley folds and glue.

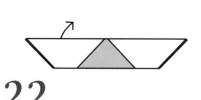

22

Unfold back layer upward.

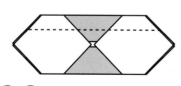

23

Valley fold.

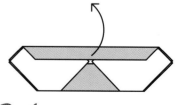

24

Unfold.

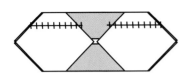

25

Cuts as shown.

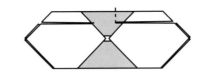

26

Valley fold.

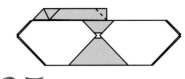

27

Valley fold.

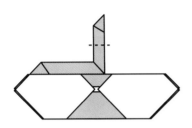

28

Valley fold.

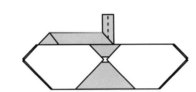

29

Valley fold.

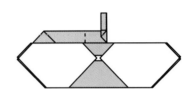

30

Valley fold.

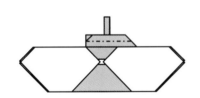

31

Squash fold.

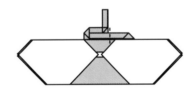

32

Inside reverse fold.

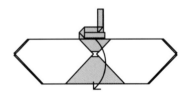

33

Valley fold.

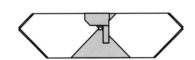

34

Unfold to a right angle, 90°.

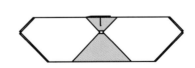

35

Add color to tower, and rotate.

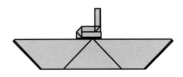

36

Completed Aircraft Carrier (see page 90 for jets).

Carrier Jets

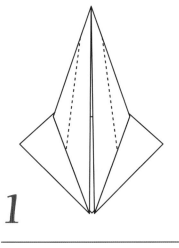

1

Start at step 11 of Base Fold III (see page 13). Valley folds.

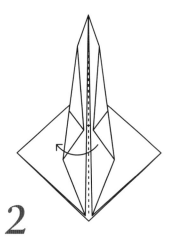

2

Valley fold.

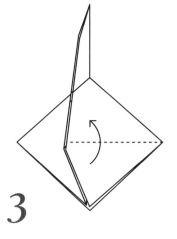

3

Valley fold.

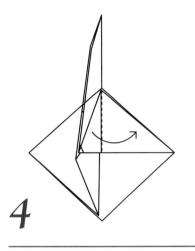

4

Valley fold.

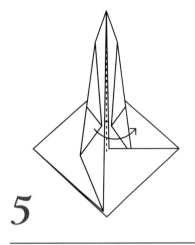

5

Valley fold.

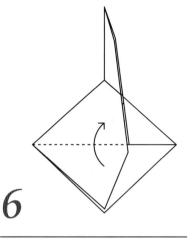

6

Valley fold.

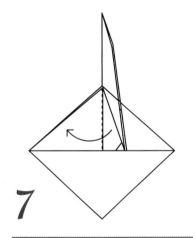

7

Valley fold.

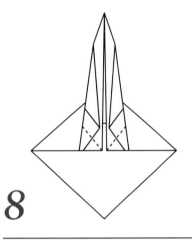

8

Valley folds.

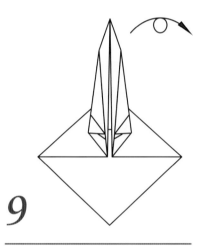

9

Turn over to other side.

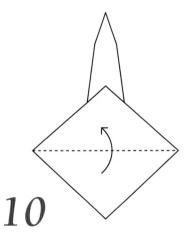

10

Valley fold.

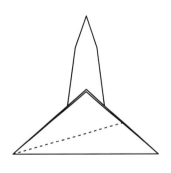

11

Valley fold.

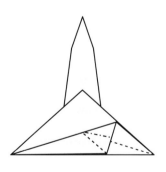

12

Inside reverse fold.

Carrier Jets

91

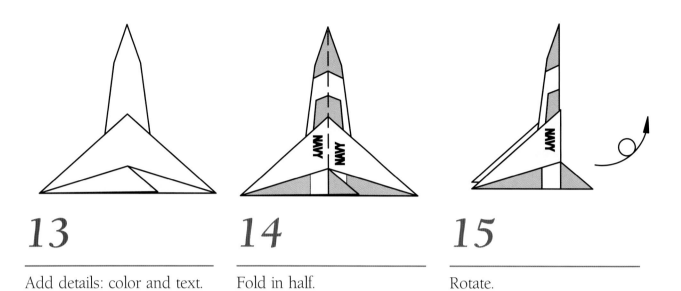

13

Add details: color and text.

14

Fold in half.

15

Rotate.

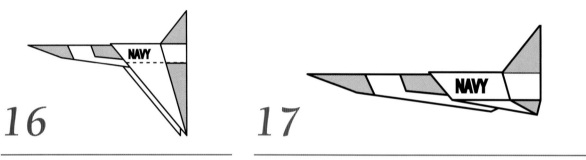

16

Valley fold wings into balanced position.

17

Completed Carrier Jet.

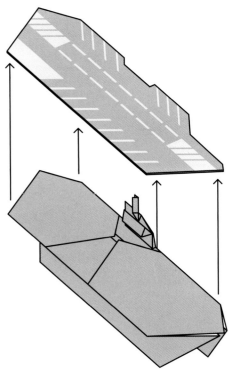

1

Place a piece of stiff cardboard against the carrier top, and cut to fit. Add detail as indicated, then position the cardboard, and glue to hold.

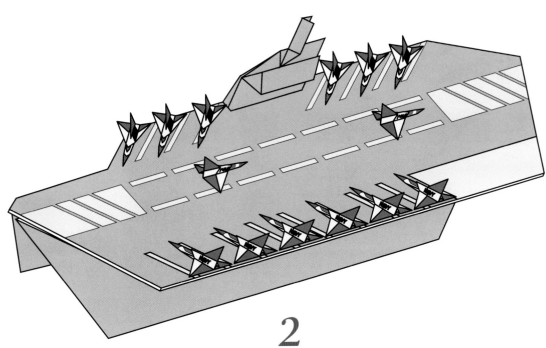

2

Add as many carrier jets as you wish for a fully outfitted Aircraft Carrier.

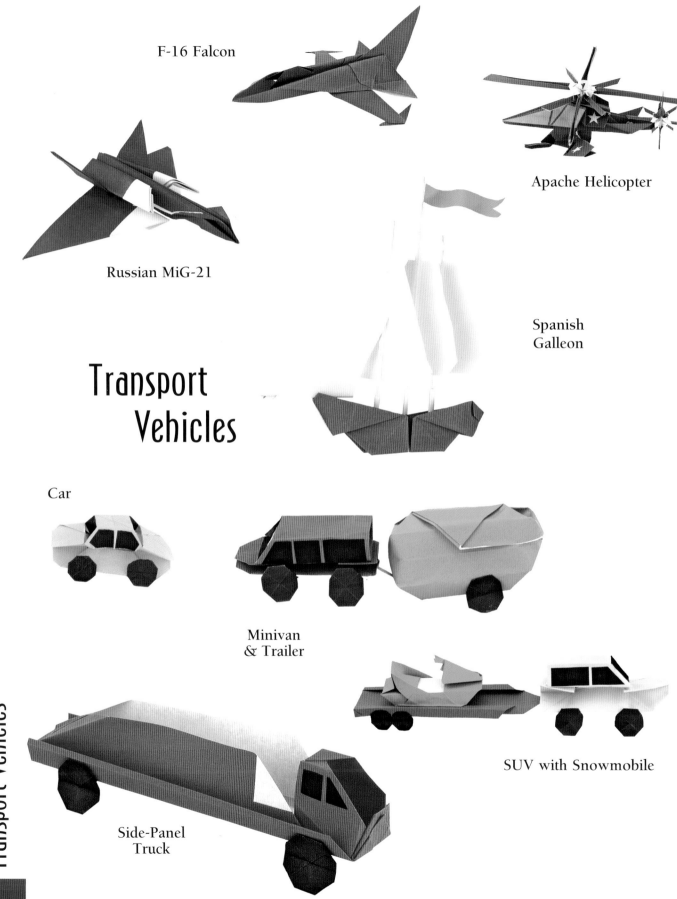

F-16 Falcon

Apache Helicopter

Russian MiG-21

Spanish
Galleon

Transport
Vehicles

Car

Minivan
& Trailer

SUV with Snowmobile

Side-Panel
Truck

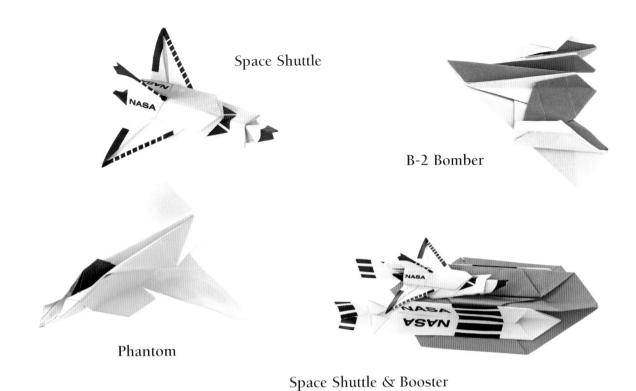

Space Shuttle

B-2 Bomber

Phantom

Space Shuttle & Booster

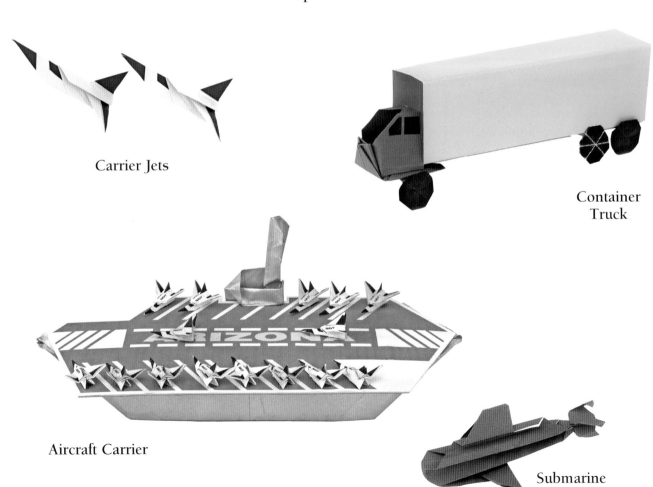

Carrier Jets

Container
Truck

Aircraft Carrier

Submarine

Index